THE
ESSENTIAL
GUIDE
TO
SPEAKING
&
LISTENING

Louis Fidge

SPEAKING & LISTENING

SPELLING

© 1992 Folens Limited, on behalf of the author.

First published 1992 by Folens Limited, Dunstable and Dublin.

Folens Limited
Albert House
Apex Business Centre
Boscombe Road
Dunstable LU5 4RL
England

ISBN 1 85276193-8

CONTENTS

CATEGORIES OF SPOKEN LANGUAGE

In the past little practical help has been available to teachers on developing spoken language but this book is intended to do just that. It sets out to provide a framework for ensuring that children do experience a rich variety of ways of using spoken language in a planned, sound, relevant and stimulating way that will be helpful to them in learning right across the curriculum.

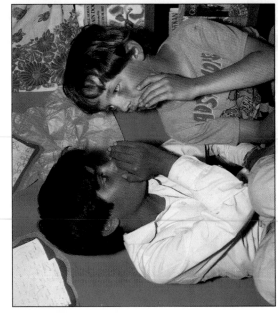

- Teachers have always been aware that 'pupils should encounter a range of situations, audiences and activities which are designed to develop their competence, precision and confidence in speaking and listening'.
- They emphasise the wide range of experiences considered necessary and stress the importance of planning for these in a systematic way.

The book is intended as a source of tried and tested practical ideas and activities for developing different aspects of spoken language and to set these in context. Key teaching points are stressed and ways of developing further activities are provided. Supporting background information and a rationale to all activities is given.

Practical advice on classroom organisation, the teacher's role and group work are spelt out and simple commonsense procedures for assessing spoken language are discussed.

Eleven different categories of spoken language have been identified and a range of suggested activities made, providing experience of each and developing them in a coherent way.

■ **Personal.** Encouraging children to express their personal feelings, ideas, concerns, opinions, views and beliefs.

■ **Descriptive.** Describing something or someone. This may be from the present, recalling from experience, or may need imagining.

■ **Narrative.** Involves creating and recounting stories or series of events in a coherent way or providing a spoken commentary to a series of events or pictures.

■ **Instructive.** Giving instructions or directions in order to effect an operation. It may involve explanatory and informative language too.

■ **Questioning.** Asking and framing questions in order to find out something.

■ **Comparative.** Comparing different things, ideas and opinions in order to make judgements based on their merits or meanings.

■ **Imaginative.** Forming mental images of objects, situations, events or people, translating these ideas into words and conveying them to others.

■ **Predictive**. Using language to predict what might happen in the future, e.g. how an event might develop, what a person might say or do as a result of what has already happened, etc.

■ **Interpretative.** Using language to explore meanings, to speculate, to make deductions and inferences.

■ **Persuasive.** Using language to change other's opinions, points of view, attitudes or to influence their behaviour in some way.

■ **Listening.** Paying attention, understanding, remembering and responding appropriately.

Separating spoken language into areas in this way is helpful as it focusses on specific ways of using talk and helps ensure that these important areas are provided for in a balanced way.

■ However, it is recognised that language is not as simple or as easy to categorise as this and that in reality all the areas interact and no one area can be taught in isolation from others. For example, speaking and listening are inextricably linked; Narrative Language will often involve Descriptive, Imaginative or Predictive elements, etc.

AN 'ENABLING' CLASSROOM ETHOS

Children should be encouraged to:

✓ evaluate, justify, clarify and explain their ideas

✓ reflect on their own learning and be self-critical

✓ listen attentively and actively

✓ offer positive, critical comments about others

✓ comment and ask questions.

Language plays a crucial role in our lives. It is important to get children to reflect on this and to raise their conscious level of awareness about the ways we use it through discussion. Speaking and listening are especially important in the classroom for learning. By discussing the value of language, particularly spoken language, we focus attention on it and raise its profile, demonstrating that we do see it as important.

Obviously the very way classrooms are organised and run will reinforce daily the value placed on language.

- Classrooms where quality speaking and listening take place are characterised by the following:
  - speaking and listening are given status and importance
  - time is given to exploring information and learning through talk.
- The classroom presents a challenging, 'thinking' context for learning.
- An investigative rather than didactic approach to learning and teaching is the norm where open-ended, exploratory talk is encouraged.
- Learning frequently takes place using problem-solving situations with real and relevant goals, and practical, identifiable outcomes.
- A rich variety of speaking and listening is encouraged, spontaneous and opportunistic, structured and planned, personal and formal.
- The classroom is a place where openness and trust are commonplace, and there is a supportive atmosphere where all contributions are valued and appreciated.
- Differing points of view are considered, listened to and weighed.
- Small, collaborative groupwork is encouraged.

The following ideas will help focus thinking from time to time. These discussion pointers may be used with larger groups or within the context of small group discussions.

■ Why is language important? What do we need it for?

■ What are the main forms of language? (Reading, Writing, Speaking, Listening.)

■ What are the main purposes of each? Why do we need them?

■ Which do we use most? Which will we need most in our lives? Why?

■ If you were only given one form of language, i.e. speaking, listening, reading, writing, which would you choose?

■ When do we use each form of language most? Where? In what situations? (Give some situations and ask which form of language is going to be most useful, e.g. you get lost, you want to cook something from a packet in the kitchen, you are involved in an accident, you want to thank your uncle for sending you a birthday present but he is not on the phone, etc ...)

■ In the past people believed that children should be seen and not heard. Victorian classrooms were very quiet places. Children were punished for talking. How would you persuade someone that talking is important in the classroom?

■ We use spoken language differently for different purposes - to explain, to describe, etc. Try to think of as many different categories as possible for using spoken language. Discuss some of the situations in which we would use different categories of spoken language.

■ Do we speak differently to different people at different times in different places?

■ What is listening? Why do we need to listen? What is a good listener? Are there different sorts of listening?

AUDIENCES AND OPPORTUNITIES FOR CHILDREN'S TALK

Flexible groupings are recommended, varying in size and composition according to the task and purpose. For example, sometimes interest groups may evolve because of something they are currently working on. Sometimes friendship groups may be appropriate (although these may generate more undirected talk unrelated to the topic than desired!). Mixed ability groups are another possibility.

- Generally, speaking and listening flourish best in small group situations which are usually set up and planned by the teacher, but not necessarily directly teacher-led.
- The skill of the teacher is in organising appropriate situations and ensuring that groups are well balanced, not dominated by certain members and that all children have a chance to participate.
- The teacher clearly plays an important role in the classroom, and will often be a participant in speaking and listening activities with the children. This may be in the context of the whole class or in small groups. The teacher will also want to create opportunities for talking with children on a one-to-one basis.

Paired work is often ideal for encouraging participation and interaction. Even children who may lack confidence or be shy are likely to respond in a one-to-one situation.

There will, of course, be many occasions when the teacher wishes or needs to talk to large groups, e.g. the whole school in assembly, year groups, his or her whole class. This is important, necessary and helpful for many reasons but is obviously not the best way of presenting opportunities for individuals to experience sustained talk. Sensitivity as to who goes with whom is of course necessary.

Children need to learn the social rules for speaking and listening in groups. They certainly learn by example but it is good to get them to talk this whole area through together. This helps to raise their awareness of the issues and express their views publicly, to negotiate and listen to others' views, and to come to some consensually agreed shared understanding.

■ One way of stimulating this is to show them, or read to them, a checklist produced by other children on the same topic. They should then discuss their own feelings and ideas in small groups. Each group could be asked to come up with a number of suggestions for a report back session or just leave it open-ended.

■ The teacher could then draw the ends together and review what has been said in different groups. Ideas could be written down and after a discussion a class list drawn up. Alternatively the list of ideas could be given back to the groups and they could be asked to rank them, or choose the most important five or ten. From this a class list could then be produced.

■ It would be good for each child to have their own copy (handwritten or word-processed and decorated by them) or a class poster could be produced and displayed prominently for reference and as a reminder.

Ten Rules For Working in Groups

1 Try to get on with the people in your group.

2 Take it in turns to speak.

3 Don't butt in - wait till the other person finishes.

4 Don't just accept everything everyone says. Listen carefully.

5 If you disagree, say so but remember to say something nice about what the other person said.

6 Ask questions if you don't understand.

7 Explain well. Keep to the point and make things clear.

8 Say things which help others.

9 Share your suggestions and ideas with the rest of the group.

10 Speak up but don't boss others around.

It is also good to create opportunities for children to be involved in talking to and with other adults in school - parents helping in the class, welfare assistants, other members of the community, etc. This may be in a variety of settings, e.g. one-to-one, small group or as a class. Similarly, planning opportunities for talk with children from other classes (of the same or different age) is good for creating a variety of audiences and purposes.

THE TEACHER'S ROLE AND ORGANISATION

- Flexibility is the keynote in terms of classroom organisation. A wide variety of approaches are possible.
- The age and ability of the children and the activity being pursued will determine the degree and the nature of the involvement.
- At times you will find yourself adopting a variety of roles.

THE ADMINISTRATOR

In this capacity you will be operating as:

✓ *The Facilitator* encouraging and organising things to promote progress

✓ *The Co-ordinator* of activities

✓ *The Time Manager* ensuring that time is not unnecessarily wasted and unproductively used

✓ *The Enabler* in making essential resources available.

THE INTERVENER

Here you take on roles as:

✓ *The Adviser* on how to approach tasks

✓ *The Observer* of progress and the need for feedback. Sometimes this will take the form of *The Silent Observer*. This is by far the most difficult role to play as it involves you standing back and observing as children work independently, making mistakes and losing their way

✓ *The Challenger* where you ask open-ended questions or challenge the children to do something

✓ *The Critic* discouraging loose and sloppy thinking

✓ *The Respondent* to children's queries

✓ *The Evaluator, Assessor and Judge* where you evaluate ideas, assessing the quality of speaking and listening and of progress made.

THE ASSOCIATE LEARNER

As well as the roles you will play from time to time, probably the most underrated of roles is that of the Associate Learner.

✓ In this role you will be working alongside children, not dominating but as a genuine co-partner in a learning enterprise.

THE LEADER

You lead discussions, guide and structure ideas, provide ideas for what is to be done and how. In this capacity you might find yourself acting as:

✓ *The Creator* of the learning environment

✓ *The Stimulator* of children's ideas

✓ *The Intermediary* in discussions with the children

✓ *The Manager* of the whole learning situation

✓ *The Presenter* of information and tasks.

With the whole class it is possible to create opportunities to raise topical issues for discussion, to talk about stories that have been read to them, to create times for sharing experiences and news, etc., but the degree of individual participation will be limited and the type and amount of talk possible restricted.

Whole class work is good for information giving and introducing new ideas and topics prior to small groupwork, so that key ideas and concepts may be introduced. Examples may be given and certain types of talk modelled and discussed. Goals can be set and tasks explained so that everyone knows what they are doing. Organisational details can be discussed.

It is possible for all the class to be working in pairs or in small groups on the same or different discussion activities if desired. Alternatively, a large group could be working on another type of learning activity whilst a small group, or a few small groups or pairs of children could be involved on some planned speaking and listening activity.

During the course of small groupwork the teacher would be managing and organising the environment, keeping things moving and checking groups are on task,

■ The teacher would probably move from group to group, encouraging, stimulating, offering help where necessary but generally keeping a fairly low profile. If teachers get too involved in the actual discussions in this sort of informal groupwork all too often the nature of the talk changes subtly, the children deferring to the teacher and the teacher leading and dominating.

■ There is, of course, a place for direct intervention. During the discussions or at the end of them, some or all of the groups can be called together as a larger group.

■ This is helpful sometimes as a way of checking collectively that everyone is on the right track. It means that different groups can share where they have got to so far and learn, and be stimulated, by other groups. Key points can be brought out if necessary. It may be that the teacher may want to introduce a new element or change tack slightly in the light of things that have emerged so that the discussions develop in a different way.

■ At the end of discussions it is also often beneficial to review what each group has come up with, to enable them to have a reporting-back session and for them to compare and evaluate each other's thoughts. The teacher can draw together loose ends and ensure that any key points are reinforced.

■ It may be that it is possible to follow up, extend or develop some of the activities with further discussion, or consolidate them by writing (posters, reports, stories and poems, etc.), art work or in many other ways.

The activities and suggestions in this book may be used with groups organised in whichever combinations of the above ways the teacher feels most appropriate. No specific guidance is given on this.

ASSESSMENT

- This book provides a range and variety of language opportunities and experiences for developing language in different contexts.
- It is useful to have a framework for assessing these. We therefore offer:
  - a Summary of Specific Language skills and
  - a Summary of General Language skills for this purpose.

The success of particular activities depends on many diverse factors. For example:

✓ The organisation and composition of the groups. Are they able to concentrate? Do they gel together? Are they too big? Are there dominant characters in them? etc.

✓ The appropriateness, relevance, and level of difficulty of the task

✓ The clarity of instructions and presentation of stimulus to the children

✓ The degree of interest and motivation shown.

Many of these factors depend on the teacher's skills in sustaining, managing, motivating, enthusing, supporting, matching tasks to children, etc. One form of assessment therefore needs to be the ability of the teacher to reflect upon his or her own skills.

Assessment of the children might be carried out at three different levels.

INFORMAL

This is the sort of daily ongoing assessment that teachers are making all the time. In terms of Speaking and Listening it will revolve around observations of children at work in different situations and making fairly subjective judgements about performance and quality of talk. The teacher will base judgements on observable features of behaviour like levels of engagement in the tasks, enthusiasm, interest shown, willingness to contribute and get involved, social behaviour, perceived quality of talking and listening, etc.

Summary of specific language skills	Name:	
DIMENSION	Good - Poor	Comments
Personal	☐ ☐ ☐ ☐ ☐	
Descriptive	☐ ☐ ☐ ☐ ☐	
Narrative	☐ ☐ ☐ ☐ ☐	
Instructive	☐ ☐ ☐ ☐ ☐	
Questioning	☐ ☐ ☐ ☐ ☐	
Comparative	☐ ☐ ☐ ☐ ☐	
Imaginative	☐ ☐ ☐ ☐ ☐	
Predictive	☐ ☐ ☐ ☐ ☐	
Interpretative	☐ ☐ ☐ ☐ ☐	
Persuasive	☐ ☐ ☐ ☐ ☐	
Listening	☐ ☐ ☐ ☐ ☐	

SEMI-FORMAL

This is where slightly more formalised approaches are used like getting groups to report back to the teacher or to the class thus enabling an idea to be gained as to how the children got on. Groups could be asked to comment on what they feel they have learned, how well they think they did and in what ways they feel they might improve.

FORMAL

A more formal approach is helpful from time to time when the teacher reflects on individual children's developing skills and competences both as an individual (by considering their development in specific areas of language, identifying strengths and weaknesses) and as an individual in different group contexts (by considering aspects of speaking and listening of a more general nature).

Assessment by the children. It is also important that children learn to reflect on their own performance and development and learn to become self-critical. Within the context of a group this can be done:

- by asking the children to review what they have done
- to comment on what has been learned
- to report back to the teacher or to share their thoughts with other groups and
- compare their ideas with those of others.

They can also be asked from time to time to comment on the performance of the group as a whole, on how well individuals contributed and shared and to consider how performance could be improved.

■ Individual children could be encouraged to reflect on their own use and understanding of language during the course of occasional one-to-one conferences with the teacher. They could also be asked to reflect on their performance by using a simple self-assessment sheet.

Summary of General Language Skills   Name: _____

DIMENSION	Pair (Good - Poor)	Small group (Good - Poor)	Child with adult (Good - Poor)	small/large group with adult (Good - Poor)	Comments
General range + range variety of language used	☐☐☐☐	☐☐☐☐	☐☐☐☐	☐☐☐☐	
Ability to speak audibly and clearly	☐☐☐☐	☐☐☐☐	☐☐☐☐	☐☐☐☐	
Ability to make self understood and structure language clearly	☐☐☐☐	☐☐☐☐	☐☐☐☐	☐☐☐☐	
Ability to adjust language according to different purposes	☐☐☐☐	☐☐☐☐	☐☐☐☐	☐☐☐☐	
Ability to reflect on own language	☐☐☐☐	☐☐☐☐	☐☐☐☐	☐☐☐☐	
Confidence	☐☐☐☐	☐☐☐☐	☐☐☐☐	☐☐☐☐	
Behaviour in group situations	☐☐☐☐	☐☐☐☐	☐☐☐☐	☐☐☐☐	
Willingness to share ideas and suggestions and join in	☐☐☐☐	☐☐☐☐	☐☐☐☐	☐☐☐☐	
Ability to take turns	☐☐☐☐	☐☐☐☐	☐☐☐☐	☐☐☐☐	
Ability to listen to others	☐☐☐☐	☐☐☐☐	☐☐☐☐	☐☐☐☐	

SPEAKING AND LISTENING ACTIVITIES

Name: _____ Date: _____

Title of activity: _____

What was the activity about? _____

Did you enjoy the activity? (Say why you give this answer.) _____

Who were you working with? _____

How did you get on? _____

Did one person do most of the talking, or did you all do about the same? _____

How good do you think you were? _____

	Tick the correct box Not very good	Alright	Good
... at talking?	☐	☐	☐
... at listening?	☐	☐	☐

Could you improve your speaking and listening in any way? How? _____

ALL ABOUT ME

Expressing our feelings and desires in spoken language is manifested in most of us right from an early age.

- Personal Language is literally all about giving of ourself in some way through talk. We are unlikely to talk freely and in this personal way if we feel uncomfortable or unsupported.
- Opportunities need to be created which are encouraging and not threatening.
- All contributions should be respected and sensitively treated.
- Children will be more prepared to contribute this kind of talk in small informal groups with other children they like and are friendly with.

Personal Language is all about sharing our individual:

- ideas and concerns
- opinions, views and beliefs.

It is used when we talk about:

- how we feel
- what we think
- what we aspire to
- what we dream about
- what we love or hate
- what we are frightened of.

Here are some ways of getting children to talk about themselves and their experiences in a fairly straightforward factual manner:

■ **There's no-one quite like me.** Get the children to share together some of the ways in which they are special. What is special about the way you look? Talk about some of the things you are good at in school. What people and places are special to you? What is your favourite food?

■ **Memories.** Recall: some of the things you did when you were very young; your earliest memory; some things that made you happy or sad; something very exciting that happened; something that worried you.

■ **Lost.** Talk about a time when you were lost. Where did it happen? Who were you with? How did it happen? How did you feel? How did it all turn out? Imagine you have gone for a walk in the woods with a friend. It is getting very late and dark. You realise you are lost. Talk about what you might do and what might happen.

Everyone has secret wishes and ambitions. Everyone dreams. Everyone imagines things. The following ideas encourage children to talk about these things personally.

■ **When I grow up.** What would you like to be when you grow up? A builder? A pop star? A doctor? A footballer? What sorts of things would you do? Where would you like to go? To the moon? To an adventure park? Somewhere else?

■ **Dreams.** What is a dream? Does everyone dream? When do you dream? How do you know if you have had a dream? Have you ever had a bad dream? What was it about? Who do you tell if you have a nightmare?

■ **Wishes.** Ask the class to write on a piece of paper what two (or three) wishes they would love to have granted. These could then be typed up and separated into single strips of paper, each with one wish on it. The group could then be given five or six of them to discuss. Which do they think are sensible? They could then try to rank them in what they consider to be an appropriate order of importance. They could follow this by talking about their own special wishes.

WHAT IS A DREAM?

DOES EVERYONE DREAM?

HOW DO YOU KNOW IF YOU HAVE HAD A DREAM?

WHEN DO YOU DREAM?

How do we respond and feel in particular situations? These activities get children talking about common experiences.

■ **Being teased.** Think of as many things as you can that people get teased about. Share your ideas with a partner or in a group. Talk about how you feel when you are teased. What do you do? Is it kind to tease? What do you do when you see someone being teased.

■ **Being left out.** Sometimes we find ourselves excluded or left out. Have you ever felt like this? When? How do you feel when it happens? What can you do? What can you do when you see someone else being left out?

■ **Being scared.** Talk to your partner about what things frighten you? People who shout? Horror films? Bullies? Something else?

PERSONAL FEELINGS AND OPINIONS

Have a general discussion with the class on moods and give children an example

'Sometimes I get in a hurrying mood. I want to get out to play so I hurry up my mum with my tea. I snatch a drink and eat my tea ever so quickly. I throw on my coat and rush out of the house. I shout goodbye loudly and run to my friend's. When I'm in a hurrying mood it makes me impatient. I want to do everything quickly. My brain feels all rushed and my heart beats fast. I can't seem to do anything slowly.'

You could talk about other moods, e.g. sulky, quiet, etc., in the same way. Ask them to come up with other sorts of moods. Write them down as a list.

Give the groups the list, e.g. angry, wild, lazy, unkind, thoughtful, annoying, loud, etc. Ask them to talk to each other about them. Talk about the sorts of things they do when in these moods, how it affects their behaviour, how it affects the way they relate to others, how it makes them feel, what is going on inside their heads and bodies, etc.

Happiness is ... Together as a class compose a list poem on the board along the happiness is ... theme, e.g. Happiness is ... putting in the last piece of the jigsaw ... sucking a cold ice lolly... stroking my puppy, etc. Talk about things that make them personally happy or things that they think would make them happy.

In groups give them a list of titles like:

- bravery is ...
- anger is ...
- trust is ...
- a secret is ...
- peace is ...
- kindness is ...
- fear is ...
- meanness is ...
- surprise is ...
- boredom is ...
- loneliness is ...
- curiosity is ...
- sorrow is ...
- excitement is ...

Get them to talk together about their own feelings on these things and then to brainstorm and come up with as many Happiness is ... - type ideas for some of them. (They could be turned into group poems and shared with others as a follow-up.)

We all have attitudes and points of views on most things. Expressing our opinions gives others an insight into what we, as individuals, think. These activities are examples of ways in which we can encourage children to share some of their personal views with others.

■ **TV preferences.** As a class discuss together children's TV preferences. Get them to explain what they like and why they like it. Draw out that not everyone shares everyone else's choices.

■ **Surveys.** Carry out some class surveys on various things, e.g. favourite (or worst!) pop groups, football teams, adverts, food, drinks, fruit, etc.

■ In groups ask them to analyse the results. Are they surprised? Are they very different from their own points of view? What do they think of the choices made? Would the results have been very different if their parents had filled out the survey forms? Why? Would the results have been different five years ago? Why? Would they still think the same in five years' time?

■ This can be tackled successfully in another way too. Ask individual children to write down their three (or more) favourite ... TV programmes, adverts, games, etc. Next they have to get together with a partner and each has to explain their choices about one of these topics - to say what they like and why. Together they then have to discuss their lists and come up with a list between them of just three or four items and rank them in order of preference. This could be further extended by getting them together with another pair and carrying out the same exercise again.

MY TOP FIVE FAVOURITE TV PROGRAMMES

work these out with your parents

ANTICIPATION

- Sometimes situations affect us in a very personal way.
- We try to anticipate these by talking them through based on our previous knowledge or experience of the context and the predicted likely outcomes.

How would you feel if ...?
What would happen if ...?
How would you respond if ...?
We often try to anticipate situations and events by talking about the consequences of them for us in a very personal way. In a sense, this enables us to empathise better with others in such situations and to plan and prepare ourselves emotionally and mentally to cope better should we ever be placed in such a situation. It may often mean using our imaginations or basing our judgements on vicarious experiences - of others, of knowledge gained through books or TV, etc.

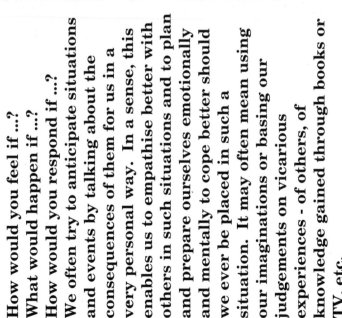

Here we consider some situations which would mean considerable changes in our personal lives. Try to anticipate how these would affect us in different ways.

Moving to a new house. If your parents told you that you were going to move to a new house in another town, what sorts of things would you immediately think of?

- How would you feel?
- What good things can you think of about moving to a new house?
- What do you think you would dislike about it?
- What do you think the problems would be for you?
- What possible reasons could you give to your parents to persuade them not to go?

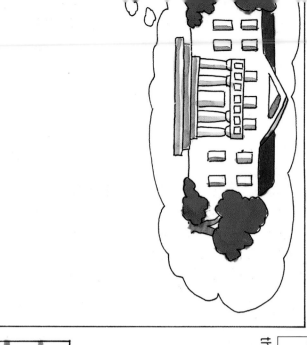

Going to the dentist. How do children feel when they have to go to the dentist? Questions to ask:

- What sort of things come into your mind when you think about it?
- What are the good things about going to the dentist?
- What are the things you really dislike about it?
- What excuses can you come up with for getting out of going to the dentist?

What would you do if ...? Get the children to imagine that on the way home from school, they see someone trying to climb in through a window, into their house.

- What do they think when they first see this person?
- What do they feel?
- What do they think about doing?

This can bring into discussion ideas about stereotypes and what children expect certain 'kinds' of people to do and say.

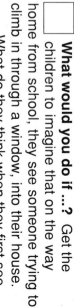

This 'What would you do if ....?' theme can be extended in an imaginative way, perhaps using role-play. Imagine you hide and watch. What happens? Imagine you try to stop this person. What does he/she say?

- *Imagine you tell someone about this 'adventure'. What do you say?*
- *Pictures of people can be usefully used here. Children can hypothesise about people in situations. Who is the person? What is his/her background?*
- *Children could describe the people to their partners.*

MAKING EXCUSES

Excuses are often a way of avoiding blame or fault, or being told off or punished. We often hear people making excuses. We all do it. But why?

I was stopped on my way home by an alien from outer space and invited to have a look around the spacecraft!

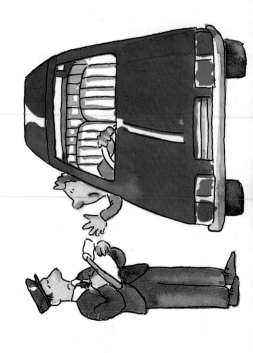

I'm sorry officer ... but I didn't see ... the red light!

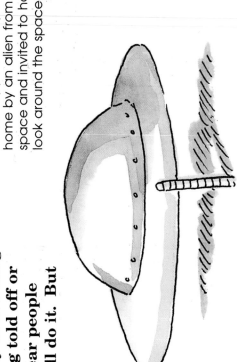

The aim of this unit is to think through some of the issues involved in making excuses.

- What are excuses?
- Why do people use them?
- What sort of language is used?
- How do people tend to speak when offering excuses, e.g. apologetically? Why?
- Are excuses always truthful?
- How do we decide what to give as an excuse?
- Do we make different sorts of excuses to different people, e.g. our friends, parents, teachers, etc?
- Do we talk differently to these different sorts of people when offering excuses?

Excuses to parents.

What sort of excuses could you give your parents for being late home from school? Think of as many believable excuses as you can to persuade your parents why you are late home from school. Then have some fun thinking up some really unbelievable excuses.

■ How many believable excuses can you think of for:

- getting your clothes muddy?
- getting out of doing the washing-up?
- not eating sprouts?

■ Excuses at school.

How many believable excuses can you come up with for:

- forgetting to do your homework?
- spilling paint on your friend's picture?
- talking in assembly when you shouldn't have?
- flicking food in the dining room?

I had to stay in after school to finish off some work.

I'm sorry but I didn't know the gun was loaded!

I'm sorry but I didn't know this tin was holding all the others up.

Some excuses are more believable than others!

☐ *Think about other situations at home or in school where excuses are often used.*

■ *Excuses to others. Think of the sorts of excuses you might give a policeman if you:*
- *were speeding*
- *went through a red traffic light.*

■ *What sort of excuses do you think librarians get when people bring their books back late?*

CREATING THE RIGHT IMPRESSION

Giving someone a good impression of something involves being selective in what you tell or show them. It involves an appreciation of what you think is good or worth showing or telling, and what you think the other person will be impressed with. It is often a subtle form of persuasion by 'selective editing'.

Creating a good impression often means putting up a pretence. It may mean 'bending the truth' somewhat by pretending to have certain qualities, e.g. to be braver than we actually are, or to do something better than we really can.

It might mean putting up an elaborate front and pretending to be better than we really are. Exaggeration is involved in persuading people. In many ways, 'creating a good impression' is tied up with our human desire to be seen in the best possible light and our need to be admired and respected.

- Creating the right impression might involve:
  - the selective use of language to show ourselves in the best possible light
  - using persuasive language to convince
  - using language which exaggerates or 'bends the truth'.

□ **Presenting yourself.** Show someone a story you have written. Explain to them all the things you think are good about it.

■ **Presenting yourself to others.** Ask the children to think and talk about how they would behave and what sort of things they would say when they want to create a good impression with:
- a new teacher
- a new child in the class
- a boy or girl they want to impress.

■ **Talking about yourself.** When you meet someone for the first time and they ask you to tell them about yourself, what sort of things do you tell them? What sort of things don't you tell them? Why?

■ **Talking about things that happen.** Has anything really frightening ever happened to you? When you tell people about it do you exaggerate a little and make yourself sound braver than you really were or make the incident sound more frightening than it really was? Why?

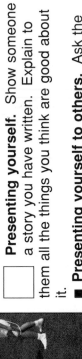

22

'Looking good'. People spend enormous amounts of money, time and energy making themselves 'look good'. Ask children to discuss some of the issues:

- what do they think about make-up?
- is it important?
- for whom - the person wearing it or other people?
- is the make-up industry really an advertiser's trick?
- should men wear make-up?
- why do people wear jewellery?
- when?
- what makes good jewellery?
- have people always worn it?
- what makes a good hairstyle?
- are there fashions in hairstyles?

■ **Dressing up and fashion.** One way of introducing this is to compare pictures of different fashions in different periods of history in order to talk about the changing face of fashion.

- Do clothes really matter?
- Do 'clothes make the man' (or woman!)?
- Why do fashions change?
- What is fashionable at the moment?
- Are different people's ideas on fashions different? Why?

■ **'Sticks and stones'.** Get children to talk about name calling.

- Why do we do it?
- How do we feel when it happens to us?
- Does it matter?

Stereotypes. This is an interesting area for discussion but needs sensitive handling. One way of introducing this is to have a variety of photographs of people. Some may be dressed well, some not. It may be clear from the photographs what people do, e.g. a doctor. Try to include people of different ages, sexes, races, social backgrounds, with different physical characteristics - glasses, thin, fat. Ask children to talk about the pictures and discuss what sort of people they think these are. Through discussion, try to raise the children's awareness of how easily and almost unconsciously we make assumptions about people based on very little evidence and how we tend to classify people according to observable characteristics.

- How can we prevent ourselves from doing this?
- What should we be looking for in people?

The visitor. *Imagine your Head Teacher has asked you to show a special visitor around the school.*

- *Where would you start?*
- *What special places would you show the visitor?*
- *What are the good places to go to?*
- *Are there any places that you would not visit? Why not?*
- *What would you say to the visitor about the places you visit?*
- *Would you go into every classroom?*
- *To whom would you introduce the visitor?*

ARGUING

Arguments are, by definition, very personal in nature. They often occur when two or more people want something they can't both have or want to do something different and can't agree about it. Arguments often involve heated emotional responses.

- There are close links between:
  - discussing
  - debating
  - arguing.
- Arguing often involves the use of persuasive language, verbal and/or non-verbal.
- Arguments usually centre around issues about which individuals feel strongly, or where the loss of prestige or self-esteem are at risk.

Here are some general issues involved in arguing.

- What sort of things do you argue over?
- What sort of things do adults argue over? Why?
- When do arguments happen? Why?
- Are arguments necessary?
- How can they be avoided?
- How do you 'get round' people and get your way without arguing?
- How do you cope with arguments?
- How do you resolve arguments?
- Is arguing the same as discussing?

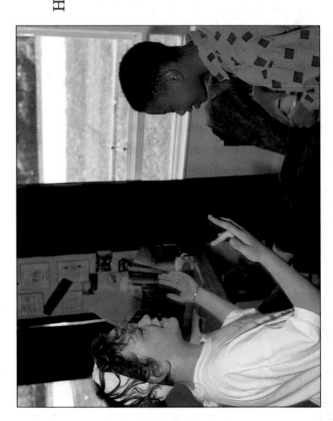

Arguing with friends. Which friends do you argue with most?

- Why?
- What do you argue about?
- Who usually starts the arguments?
- Who usually finishes them?
- How?
- Do you ever argue very much with children you do not like?
- Why?

■ **Arguing in the playground.** What sort of arguments are there on the playground?

- Who causes them?
- Do girls argue more than boys?
- Do boys and girls argue about different things?

■ **Arguing at home.** Do you ever argue at home.

- With whom?
- What sort of things do you argue about?
- How do you feel when you argue?
- What five things can you do to prevent arguments?

yes.

■ *Formal debates.* Arguing, debating and discussing are often very similar. Depending on the age of the children, it might be appropriate to consider having a more formal debate on a topic, e.g. school uniform, speed limits, whale hunting. The danger of debates is that children often have insufficient information to enable them to make meaningful judgements. Prior to any debate it would be helpful to have a 'fact-finding' lesson so that children can be better prepared. It may well be that a class debate is the most useful starting point so that you, as a teacher, could support, encourage and keep things going where necessary.

USING YOUR EYES

We most often associate descriptive language with writing. We are used to encouraging children to use it in this form. One way of getting children to reflect on the use of this aspect of language is to use this as a starting point and to approach it initially through literature, by reading passages and discussing the author's use of words, the effectiveness of the language, the vividness of the descriptions.

These sort of discussions are perhaps best done in the whole class context, although sometimes you may find it helpful in small group situations. It is helpful to compare the writer's craft with that of the artist. Whereas the artist uses a brush and paints to create a picture, the writer has to use words.

Creating meaningful and relevant opportunities for using spoken descriptive language is not the easiest of tasks. A very effective way of doing this, and maintaining interest and fun is through games and challenges. The following ideas are best carried out in small groups, preferably in pairs, although some may lend themselves to other styles of organisation.

- To be effective, careful, accurate observation is necessary.
- When describing select the key features first. This is a good way of getting your message across.
- Reflective and careful choice of words is important.
- The test of a good description is how well the listener is able to build up a picture of what is being described.
- Descriptive language requires good interactive listening skills too. It is important to concentrate on listening.

Descriptive language is all about the effective use of words. The following activities are a few of the many possible ways of encouraging children to develop more effective use of words when describing things. The activities are all based around a theme of our five senses.

The animal game. You need lots of pictures of different animals:

- Spread out the pictures so they are visible to both children.
- Partner 1 chooses an animal (without letting Partner 2 know which one has been selected).
- Partner 1 describes one or two characteristics of the animal, e.g. it has four legs and a short tail. Partner 2 tries to guess, if necessary being given more and more clues.
- How many clues does it take?
- The partners then swap roles.

A third person could be involved as an 'auditor', to sit in and observe and comment on how they feel the describer did. They could comment on the quality of the description and how it might have been improved. The same principle used for the animal game can be applied to any collection of pictures - of people, groups of things, e.g. transport, situations, events, etc.

■ **Describe a friend.** Each partner has to choose someone in the class. In turns they describe the person's characteristics until the partner has guessed who is being described. Teachers could be chosen, or anyone else who works at the school.

■ Another variation of this is to ask children to describe someone they know very well. It could be a parent, a relative, etc. The partner does not necessarily have to know the person but has to comment on what they thought of the description and what they liked about it. This could be extended to describing places they like to visit, etc.

■ **Making a 'wanted' poster.** A further activity along these lines is to pretend that someone both children know well is wanted by the police. They have to decide what physical characteristics of the person are important and create a sufficiently accurate description of the person to enable someone else to recognise him or her. This is an opportunity for collaborative decision-making. The resulting description could be written down and an accompanying 'wanted' poster drawn. Support may need to be given to offer some children a framework for structuring their descriptions.

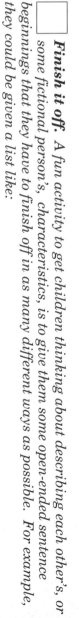

Finish it off. A fun activity to get children thinking about describing each other's, or some fictional person's, characteristics, is to give them some open-ended sentence beginnings that they have to finish off in as many different ways as possible. For example, they could be given a list like:

- My hair is like ...
- My eyes are like ...
- My feet are like ..., etc.

Some discussion is necessary to introduce the idea. You could concentrate on one aspect like the hair and give some ideas of the sort of descriptive language you want to encourage, e.g. ... like a silken waterfall, ... like shiny thread, ... like old bootlaces, ... like a greasy plate of spaghetti.

■ They then compile as many examples of each as they can. These can be written down if appropriate. They can then be shared with the other children. The best of the examples can then be made up into an identikit description of an unusual nature!

■ To simplify this the children could be given the sentence beginnings on slips of paper and a variety of sentence endings on other slips. They could discuss the appropriateness of the endings and match up those which they felt best fitted each beginning.

■ *How much do you remember?* For this the children will need a fairly 'busy' picture with lots of things happening. Get the children to discuss the picture and look at it for a few minutes. Partner 1 then has to try and describe as much about the picture as possible without looking at it. (Partner 2 has it to refer to.) The roles can then be reversed.

EFFECTIVE USE OF WORDS

This is what descriptive language is really all about. The following activities are a few of the many possible ways of encouraging children to develop more effective use of words when describing things, based on our five senses.

Many of the ideas already discussed have been very much connected with the visual. We now turn to a few ideas based around our other four senses: taste, smell, touch and hearing.

TASTY
DELICIOUS
APPETISING CRUNCHY

Taste. How would you describe the taste of things to someone who has never experienced them, e.g. a person from another planet? Examples could be given before children tried some themselves, e.g. Coke tastes sweet. It is fizzy and bubbly. Sometimes it makes you burp! Jelly is wobbly and tastes fruity. It slips down very easily.

■ Children could be given a list of things to describe in this way. Their descriptions could be illustrated as an extension activity, to assist the description.

■ An alternative is to ask children to base this on their favourite food and drinks, and their least favourite ones.

■ **Blindfolded tasting sessions.** Great fun! Prepare several saucers of different foods, e.g. tomato sauce, cut-up apple, mustard, pickle, etc. Children are blindfolded so they can't see what they are tasting. They are not allowed to say what it is they think they are tasting but try to describe it in other ways.

Go on spoil yourself

Try our SUPER-SPECIAL Extra-Flaky Chocolate-Bar

YOU WILL NEVER BE THE SAME AGAIN!

FLAKY CHOK BAR

■ **Hearing.** Start off by getting the children to close their eyes and to listen carefully to the sounds around them for a minute. Get the children then to say what they heard. Encourage them to respond using descriptive language, e.g. the rustling of paper, the shuffle of feet, the clicking of heels, etc.

■ *This can be developed by asking them to imagine different scenarios, e.g. they are laying in bed in the morning (the sound of the chink of the milkman's bottles, the running of a tap, etc.) or at night before everyone else has gone to bed (the creak of the stairs, the quiet voices of the TV).*

■ *Pictures are a good way of working their imaginations, e.g. a picture of a busy seaside beach, firework night, etc. Together they could list all the sounds they might possibly hear.*

■ *This could be developed by reading a passage about an animal in the jungle, a visit to the fair, etc. Children could then be asked to imagine they were there. What sounds would they hear?*

■ **Smells.** This is a more difficult topic but one way in is to ask children collectively to come up with a list of their favourite smells, e.g. bacon frying, freshly cut grass, etc. and their worst smells, e.g. smoke from bonfires, petrol and try to describe what it is they like or dislike about them.

■ **Touch.** The blindfold idea can be used again in this context but this time using a variety of objects to identify by touch alone. Children are not allowed to guess what the object actually is, but are to work hard to use descriptive language to describe how it feels, e.g. a comb ... smooth and shiny, polished in places ... a line of long, sharp spikes or teeth which are very close together, etc.

■ *This could be developed by asking children to use their imaginations and imagine they were in certain situations, e.g. their home at night when all electricity had failed and they had to find their way about by touch. What would all the everyday things that they are used to seeing, feel like? A wood at night where they couldn't see clearly but had to find their way by feeling. What would they experience?*

■ **Comparison.** Use the 'spaghetti is like ... slimy string' sort of approach where children are given a list of different foods and drinks, but this time they have to liken the food or drink to something else.

■ **Advertising.** Advertisers and shopkeepers use words cleverly too, to try and persuade people to buy food and drink, e.g. Granny Smith's Apples - crisp, juicy and crunchy; Bread - home baked and crusty. Healthy, wholemeal loaves, full of fibre and goodness. Children could be asked to think about what signs they might use to put in their shop window to encourage people to buy various items. See other ideas in Persuasive Language.

USE YOUR IMAGINATION

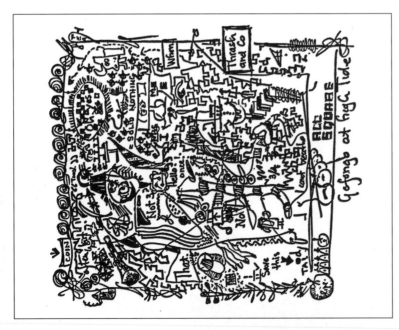

The Gofongo, if you please,
Is a fish with singing knees
And a tail that plays
The Spanish clarionet!

He has toes that whistle tunes
And explode! Like toy balloons.
Hence his many,
Many visits to the vet.

The Gofongo, when he likes,
Swallows jam and rusty bikes,
Orange pips and treacle
Pudding boiled in glue.

He loves chips with rusty nails
And can swallow iron nails
That is why they cannot keep one
in a zoo.

But! Gofongo as a pet
Would cause panic and regret.
People tried it and were
Nearly driven balmy.

For, once inside a house,
He screams, 'I'm a Jewish mouse.'
And joins the Arab army!

Spike Milligan

'**Prefabulous animiles**'. Read poems or books about imaginary animals (or simply talk about them), e.g. James Reeves 'Prefabulous animiles' or some of the Spike Milligan ideas. The task is then for the groups to create their own version of an imaginary animal through discussion. They may need to be given a framework to work within, e.g. a set of characteristics to think about (name, features, habits, what it eats, etc.). The groups then discuss ideas and produce a single version of an animal from their collective imagination. This could be written down if desired. Groups can then share their ideas and compare and discuss outcomes.

These activities move on from fairly concrete experiences to more imaginary ones. They are collaborative opportunities to create descriptions of people, events, animals, etc., from the imagination. There are clear links here with Imaginative Language.

■ **The elephant.** Another idea is to read the story about the six blind people who were asked to say what they thought an elephant was like. They were each only allowed to touch one part of the elephant. One touched the trunk, one the tail and so on. Their descriptions reflected this. The one who held the tail said an elephant was like a stiff whip. Different pictures of animals could be given to children and they could imagine they were blind and only able to touch a particular part of each animal. What would their description of the animal then be?

■ **Imaginary characters.** Characters from fairy stories are good for this. After some sort of stimulus, read, spoken or seen, children could be given a character to create. A scenario could be given to set the scene if necessary, e.g. The princess was taken by the evil giant and locked up in the high tower. Describe what they think the characters are like, how they look, what they feel, how they behave, etc. Again, the degree of support and guidance that would need to be given would depend on the age and ability of the children.

■ **My monster.** The 'My monster' idea is a great idea for encouraging accurate observational description and then leading the children into imaginary descriptions. Produce a picture of a 'fantastic' monster. Children work in pairs. Only one partner has the picture and has to describe it carefully to the other, who draws what s/he thinks is being described. Both versions are compared and differences discussed. The importance of careful description and awareness of audience are central here.

The Blind Men and the Elephant

It was six men of Indostan,
To learning much inclined,
Who went to see the Elephant
(Though all of them were blind),
That each by observation
Might satisfy his mind.

The first approached the elephant,
And happening to fall
Against his broad and sturdy side,
At once began to bawl,
'God bless me! but the elephant
Is very like a wall!' ...

Anon

Finish it off. The idea from above can also be applied to fictional characters or creatures. Children can just be given some sentence beginnings like *The wolf* ..., *the wizard was* ..., *the princess is* ..., *the knight was* ..., etc.

■ *Simple list poems.* These are a good stimulus for thinking descriptively too, e.g. *Hands are for* ... *waving goodbye, stroking a cat, polishing the car*, etc. More abstract themes like, e.g. *Happiness is* ... could also be used.

Since time immemorial the oral tradition of story-telling has been very strong, particularly in pre-literate societies. Indeed, a society's very cultural heritage and traditions have often been passed down to different generations in this way. In our Western society we have come to place less emphasis on spoken narrative language and increasingly more on writing and reading stories rather than telling them. Yet spoken narrative language is a potent form of communication and individual expression.

Aboriginal wall paintings telling stories.

- Narrative language involves creating and recounting stories or series of events in a coherent way, or retelling stories in your own words.
- It can also mean providing a spoken commentary to a series of events or pictures.
- To get children to think about story-telling, it is important to focus on the ingredients of a good story and what makes a good story-teller.

Some types of narrative language involve a willingness to play with words and ideas, to be imaginative and creative. Narrative language has close links with other aspects of language, particularly imaginative, descriptive, explanatory and predictive.

The provision of good 'models' of narrative language being used well is very important for creating a supportive, encouraging environment. A regular diet of hearing stories well read, with expression and meaning is helpful. To experience the craft of story-telling first hand, to hear and see stories being made up and well told, is better still.

Being exposed to a wide range of literature, having opportunities for absorbing different authors' styles and genres of stories, being involved in discussing what they have heard and read are all vital experiences that help children appreciate different aspects of narrative language.

RAVI AT THE FUN-FAIR

0 216 92837 0

Written and illustrated by Errol Lloyd

255×200mm · 32pp · Ages 3-6 · £6.95 · May · (w)

Naughty Ravi goes to the fun-fair with his granny and keeps disappearing. Everything is fun until he decides to go on the ghost train and suddenly realises it's best to stick with granny after all.

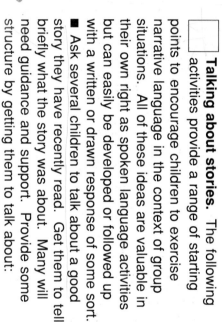

by Gemma Green
illustrated by Mrs
C A Morris

■ Talking about stories.

The following activities provide a range of starting points to encourage children to exercise narrative language in the context of group situations. All of these ideas are valuable in their own right as spoken language activities but can easily be developed or followed up with a written or drawn response of some sort.

■ Ask several children to talk about a good story they have recently read. Get them to tell briefly what the story was about. Many will need guidance and support. Provide some structure by getting them to talk about:

- the main characters (who they were, what they were like, etc.)
- where the action took place (the setting)
- an outline of what happened (the plot).

Ask them what they liked about the story and why. Ask them about the author's style and way he or she wrote, the effectiveness of the language, etc.

■ Try to get children to articulate what sort of things they like to read. What sort of books they enjoy. Try to get them to reflect on what it is about these books that they like. Is there any consensus about what makes a good book?

■ Talking about story-telling.

In the same sort of way get them to talk about the art of story-telling.

■ Why are some people boring to listen to? Why do some children fidget and not listen to stories?

■ What things make you listen during story time?

■ What people are good story-tellers?

■ What is it about them, or the way they tell stories, that makes them special?

■ How are stories best told - when they are made up, when they are remembered and retold, or when they are read from books? Or doesn't it make a difference?

RETELLING STORIES

The objectives of this unit are that children should:
- be able to listen attentively
- be able to recall the main ideas of a story - the theme, the plot, the characters, the setting
- be able to tell the story in an appropriate way for the listener, using appropriate language
- be able to present the story with expression, in a coherent way.

These activities represent three variations on a theme:

✓ **Retelling a story that has just been told or read.**

✓ **Retelling a story the children themselves have read recently.**

✓ **Retelling a traditional and familiar story read to them some time in the past.**

Telling or retelling stories is often far more effective than simply reading them. It allows for greater freedom of and movement, of gesture and interpretation.

Asking children to retell stories they have been read or told is one way of checking on how well they have been listened to or understood.

Retelling stories is an effective way of encouraging children to interpret and redefine material in their own personal way, to summarise or develop themes, plots and ideas, to play out the characters and to help them better understand the art of story-telling and interacting with an audience.

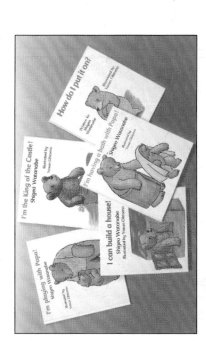

Retelling a story the children have been read or told. Read or tell a short story which is appropriate to the age and interest of the children, and not too long to sustain interest in one sitting. You may wish to show one being read or told, e.g. video.

■ Explain that you are going to ask them to retell it to each other afterwards (to encourage them to attend!). You may, or may not, wish to discuss aspects of the story after you have finished as a way of drawing out the main points or explaining any difficult parts.

■ In pairs, or small groups ask the children to retell the story. This can be done in a couple of ways:

- Explain that it is to be a group effort and that they are to help each other out.
- Ask one child to retell the story. The partner or rest of the group are to help him/her out only if stuck. The rest of the group can then be asked to comment on how well remembered the content was and on aspects of presentation. The degree of support and guidance given on this will depend on age and experience of this type of task.

☐ **Retelling a story the children have read themselves.** Ask the children in the class to retell a partner a story they have recently read. It may be a good idea to give some prior notice of this activity to enable the children to think about the task and prepare themselves a little. Explain that you want them to share their thoughts on how well their partner told the story, i.e. how much they understood, how clear the story was, how well it was presented, etc.

☐ **Retelling a traditional story.** Write down the names of several well-known stories, e.g. The Three Billy Goats Gruff, Hansel and Gretel, Little Red Riding Hood, Jack and the Beanstalk. Give them to a group of children face down and get one of them to choose one. As a group they must try to retell the story.

PICTURE STORIES

Using pictures is a good way to support narrative language.

SHUT THE GATE! 0 216 92782 X

Sonia Devons
Illustrated in full colour by Shoo Rayner

John lives on a farm. One day he decides to go for a walk. "Don't forget to shut the gate," he's told — but that is exactly what he does do with disastrous results....

203×246mm · 32pp · Ages 3-6 · £5.95 · May · (w)

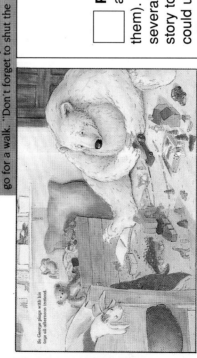

IS THAT YOU, GEORGE? 0 216 92784 6

Written and illustrated by Kate Oliver

'Is that you, George?' asks Dad nervously. Yesterday George was an ordinary little boy. Today he seems to be a large polar bear....

A delightfully funny picture book story by talented young artist, Kate Oliver.

237×195mm · 32pp · Ages 3-7 · £6.95 · April · (w)

- Using picture stories as suggested in this unit encourages:
  - careful observation
  - ability to sequence pictures to make a coherent series of events
  - ability to bring two-dimensional characters and situations to life and 'flesh them out'.

☐ **Picture books.** Ask a child to choose a picture story book (or provide one for them). Get the child to 'read' it quietly first several times. The idea is then to tell the story to a friend or small group. The child could use the book to 'read' and show, or try telling the story without the support of the book. The others in the group can then comment on what they thought of the story and the story-telling.

■ **Picture story sequences.** Photocopy a page from a picture story book or provide the children with a series of pictures (six or so depending on the age of the children) which tell a story. Cut the pictures up separately and ask the group to organise them in such a way as to tell a story. Get them then to make up a commentary for the story, giving the characters names, filling out details, etc. Get the different groups to share their outcomes and discuss any different versions that evolve. It is interesting to compare versions and discuss the merits of each.

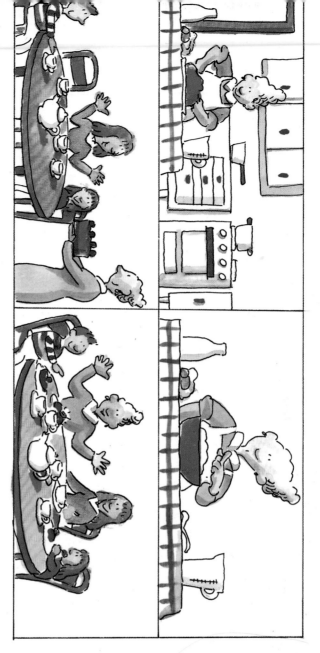

■ **Pictures of unconnected items, situations or people.** Give the group a set of six or eight pictures you have collected. They could be from magazines or drawn. They could be of different characters, or situations or scenes, or of different items. They could be a mixture of any of these. The idea is that the group collectively has to create a story which brings in all the things shown on the pictures. There must be a credible story line which should have a beginning, middle and resolution. Ask groups to share their different outcomes and discuss.

Developing a story from a single picture. After lots of experience with this sort of activity, try giving the group just one picture which has lots of things happening in it. Get the children to describe everything that is happening, to give the characters' names, to discuss why they are there, where they have come from, what has happened just before, and to try to develop the ideas by considering what might happen immediately afterwards.

■ **Picture stories with missing endings.** Give the group a few pictures detailing only the beginning of the story, e.g. how will it end? The group then has to tell the story, set the scene and decide how the story should continue. Again getting different groups to compare results is an interesting additional activity.

■ **Picture stories with missing beginnings.** This can be varied by providing the ending of a story in picture form and getting the children to supply the beginning. Recent research has shown that this method is the more successful in the production of effective communication.

EVERY PICTURE TELLS A STORY!

The context, or situation, determines what people are likely to say or do within a limited range of options. Sequences of pictures have considerable value in supporting the telling of stories or parts of stories, and as a basis for encouraging predictive language. Predictive language is used a lot in story-telling, and in listening to and reading stories.

- This section aims to use the ideas below and other similar pictorial stimuli.
- Discuss picture stimuli and predict what they think various characters might be saying, thinking, feeling.
- Use pictorial clues to guess what might have happened before or to predict what is likely to happen next.

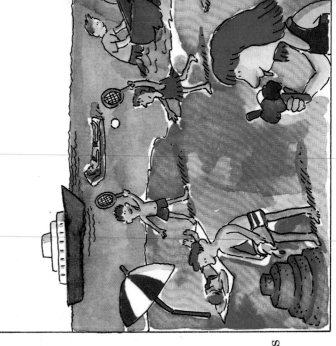

The number of pictures in the sequence and complexity of the storyline can be adjusted according to the age and ability of the children.

Different aspects of the story can be left out to encourage predictive language, e.g. the ending, the beginning or the middle.

The pictures can be presented one at a time to encourage maximum use of prediction with the minimum number of clues being given immediately. In this way children can be asked to discuss what is happening in each picture and predict what is likely to happen next. The story then gradually builds up a little at a time.

Alternatively the whole sequence you wish to show can be presented at once to give a more comprehensive overview of the story in one go. Children can then be asked to discuss what the characters are doing, what they might be saying or feeling and to predict what happens next.

The focus should be on the context of the story, the role the characters are playing in the story and predicting on the basis of this evidence what the characters might say or how they are likely to behave in such circumstances.

The Seaside. In small mixed groups of 2-4 look at a picture like the one on these pages.

- Talk about what you think the people in it might be saying and about some of the things that might happen. Some of the things might be very obvious.
- Try to think of some unexpected things that could happen.
- Decide whether the things are funny, dangerous, very unexpected, etc.
- Draw some of the things that might happen. Get children to discuss their seaside experiences and things that have happened to them, as well as encouraging them to consider things which could happen there.

■ Use photographs or pictures from books to stimulate discussions on what the people in them might happen next. Cartoons are very good for this too.

■ Use pictures and try to imagine what the people in them might be saying - perhaps children could fill in empty speech bubbles with what they think ...

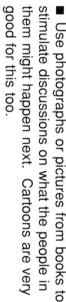

■ **How will it end?** Look at the pictures and talk about the story it tells.

- Give the children names.
- What has happened to the dog?
- What should the children do?
- How do you think the story will end?
- Can you make up some different possible endings for it?
- Decide which ending you think is best.
- Turn the pictures face down and try to retell the story together.

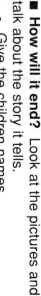

Cut up and make other picture story sequences like this. Some ideas for stories are:

Snow scene, going out, sledging, walking on frozen pond ...

Country scene, walking, see bees, follow to hive, investigate ...

Kitchen, making cake, yawn, sit in chair, sleep, forget cake ...

■ Comic strips and picture books are very good in this respect.

■ Nursery rhymes and well-known stories can be retold in pictures with the ending missing.

GIVING A FRAMEWORK

Providing some sort of model or framework is helpful in supporting and encouraging narrative language.

- In speaking and listening situations children should be prepared to:
  - consider all the given options
  - be adventurous and imaginative
  - listen to other people's suggestions.

Behaving in character. You could read the children a passage or story about a particular person or make one up, e.g. a character from a famous book or film. Talk to children about the particular character and what characteristics or personality traits he or she has. Discuss how they are likely to behave in certain situations. You could then give the group a situation and ask them to create a story featuring the character, thinking about how they would respond and deal with things, e.g. you could talk about Jonah who seems to be jinxed wherever he goes or whatever he does. His days are full of problems and catastrophes from morning till night. Tell the children about Jonah's Saturday. Ask each group to create a different day in the life of luckless Jonah. Share together each other's versions!

Setting a problem. The following is an example of the sort of possibilities. The permutations are endless and can be as simple or as complicated as appropriate.

> Anna and John are playing with a ball in the garden. It accidentally goes over the fence into the neighbour's garden. Mr Evans, their neighbour, is an old, grumpy man who is always telling them off. Anna and John are scared of him. They decide to wait till dark before going over the fence to get the ball back so they don't see Mr Evans. That night, with their hearts in their mouths, they creep over the fence and look for the ball. It is right near the window. As they stoop down to get it they see Mr Evans lying on the kitchen floor with blood on his forehead ...

The group have to discuss how he got there and what the children should do. There are many possibilities and they should try to come up with as many different ideas as possible. They could perhaps vote on which one they like best and share their ideas with other groups.

Using prepared pictures or lists.

Have five cards of the same size with pictures drawn on one side - one character and four different objects. Place the cards face down on the table except for the character card. Ask the group to say who the character is, what sort of person he or she is, and give some background. Explain that the idea is to turn up one card at a time and weave the objects into a continuing story. It should be a group effort, discussing and rejecting various possibilities and selecting together the choices that they collectively think make the best storyline.

■ **Self-service.** Produce four lists as the ones here. Working in pairs get the children to choose one or two from each list and make up a story with them. The possibilities and variations are great! Get the children to discuss their stories and think about ways of developing or improving them. This can be done by groups sharing their stories together and commenting on each other's.

Characters - real people
boy, girl, mother, father, dentist, gardener, teacher, soldier, king, queen, shopkeeper, racing driver, etc.

Characters - imaginary
wizard, goblin, unicorn, dragon, magic bird, flying horse, a cat who can change into a lion, robot, alien from space, giant, etc.

Settings
Park, street, empty house, playground, castle, cave, wood or forest, outer space, etc.

Objects
Whistle, ball, secret message, old chest, torch or lantern, book, old photograph, rope, etc.

Events
being captured, going on a journey, getting lost, something goes missing, a visitor arrives unexpectedly, weird noises are heard, everything seems different, etc.

Open-ended ways of getting children telling stories.

These ideas rely on much less support being given and therefore would be most appropriate for children who have had plenty of experience of being involved in creating stories using narrative language in group situations.

■ Read the children the beginning paragraph or two of a story. It could be just a sentence or two. Some pointers or questions could be given if appropriate, e.g. *Joanne decides to take Rover for a walk. They go down the road past the empty house. Rover begins to bark ...* Ask them to continue the story in their groups.

■ You could just give children the ending of a story in a similar way and ask them to create the rest.

■ Give the children just an idea, e.g. two children get lost; a flying dragon causes havoc to the village; there are strange sights on the castle battlements, etc.

■ Ask some 'What would happen ...' or 'What if ...' questions, e.g. What would happen if there was a sudden outbreak of blackcurrant jelly-throwing in the town centre? What if all the clouds descended to ground level?, etc.

CREATING A GROUP STORY

Group story-telling is a powerful way to use narrative and predictive language. It can be encouraged at all levels from the youngest child on. Here we concentrate especially on the predictive use of language in the process.

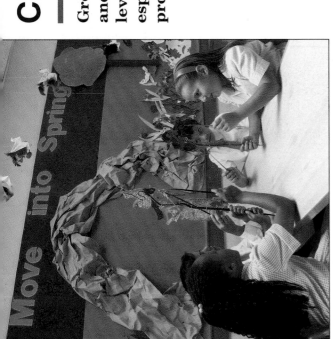

- We use prediction in reading stories all the time. But that is another story in itself and not within the scope of this book! Predictive talk can be used in story-telling and, with skilful teaching, can be encouraged when children are listening to stories being read.

The following assignment is an example of the sorts of ways in which narrative and predictive language can be developed through the medium of group story-telling and the sorts of strategies that can be used.

The parameters within which the story can develop are set. Close attention to the story context is important to appreciate the setting of the story, and to learn about the characters and the important facts which limit the range of possible ways the story can go.

When composing a group story negotiation of meaning and the choice of possible alternative ways of developing the story plays an essential part.

Listening carefully to other people's ideas and views is important.

Giving proper weight to everyone's contributions should be a priority.

Deciding upon the best option presents a good opportunity for developing and exercising persuasive language.

You may well wish to introduce the idea to the class as a whole first and discuss the task generally to ensure the task is properly understood and the ground rules are clear. The activity is then best worked in small mixed ability groups of 2-4. The reading of the prepared written part of the story is best done by a fairly competent reader, or you may wish to read it to the class yourself.

A Shock for Shiva on Planet Vulcan.
Read, discuss and finish off this story.

Explorer 2 touched down on Planet Vulcan. The crew switched on the scanner and looked out at the rocky landscape.

'It looks pretty unfriendly to me,' Shiva whispered. She clutched her transformer tightly.

Shiva was a scientist and a member of the crew of Explorer 2 who were exploring the unknown planets of the galaxy. It was her task to venture out onto Vulcan and undertake some scientific experiments whilst the rest of the crew stayed in the spacecraft. She carried the transformer in case of emergencies. There was enough power in it to give her an extra charge of superhuman power to help her get out of difficulties.

Her friends patted her on the back and wished her luck as she stepped down on to the surface of the planet Vulcan. Shiva gave a slight shudder as she had the distinct feeling that trouble lay ahead. She shrugged her shoulders and set off towards the mountains in the distance. All the time Shiva had the strange feeling she was being watched.

Suddenly, from out of nowhere a huge hairy alien appeared. Shiva's heart pounded. There was nowhere to run. Her hand grasped the transformer. 'She pressed the switch and immediately felt a surge of power racing through her body.

■ Get children to talk about what they think happens next and how Shiva manages to outwit the alien.

Shiva's heart began to return to normal again and she felt her body relax. She did not want to go through that sort of experience again. One alien was quite enough for one day!

She threw her transformer to one side. 'That's no good to me now,' she said to herself. Shiva felt a little braver and more confident now. She decided to carry on for a while ... but that was to turn out to be a bad mistake. She had only gone a short way when she found herself face to face with an even bigger, uglier, hairier creature. Shiva went to grab her transformer. Her heart sank when she remembered she no longer had it. It was just her and this ugly brute. There was noone to help her ... or was there?

■ Get the children to talk about what they think happens to Shiva. It is even more interesting if they know how the story has to carry on afterwards. One group could read this the final section ...

Shiva staggered back to the spacecraft and fell into the open door.

'Get out of here fast,' she gasped.

An angry roar came from outside and a huge black shape loomed into view. Was it too late to save the crew of the Explorer 2?

■ Children can talk about different ways in which the story could end and and choose which one they think is the best.

■ It is important for the children to listen to the different versions of the story other groups have made up. What do you think of them? How do they compare?

Talk about TV series that are left each week as cliff-hangers.

■ *Introduce the idea of chapters in reading and writing and talk about the purpose they serve.*

■ *Provide children with just the beginning or ending of a story. As a group they have to complete it.*

■ *Story chains. Each child gives a sentence. The next child carries on. How far can children get with a story before the chain breaks? Why does it break?*

INSTRUCTING

Instructive language often involves giving instructions or directions in order to effect an operation, e.g. First you have to … Turn right into … Lift the lever … Instructive language often requires a response from the listener. The listener has to use 'reactive listening skills' in order to respond appropriately.

- The effectiveness of instructive language depends on:
  - the speaker's ability to structure the information appropriately according to the listener's previous knowledge and experience
  - the listener's level of language competence
  - how well the listener is able to understand the instructions (often demonstrated through verbal or other responses).

Giving instructions - seated activities.
Give the children a simple outline picture. The children then have to give their partners several things to add to the picture, e.g. draw a tree near the house. Make the door of the house red. Draw someone looking out of the upstairs window. Stress that the child giving the instructions is only allowed to give them once!

■ This could be developed by giving children a pattern to colour in (or complete). Without pointing or touching in any way, one child has to instruct another what and how to colour in, or complete, e.g. colour the second square on the top line blue; after the third circle in the sixth line draw a small triangle.

■ **Making a model.** Using model building blocks, one child could try to get the partner making a simple model by giving verbal instructions only. No pointing, touching pieces or giving any other help is allowed. Get the children to discuss with other groups what they have discovered from this activity.

Instructive language is usually informative and explanatory. When using instructive language the speaker is often informing someone about something, or explaining to someone how to do something.

It can take the form of:
- directing or instructing someone to do something
- structuring an operation with a view to making it easier
- clarifying something
- explaining the facts about something or how to do something.

Giving instructions - moving about.

Working in pairs, ask the children to give each other three simple instructions to carry out, e.g. go to the blackboard, take the red chalk and put it on the teacher's desk. Give the groups some ideas to get them going and then ask them to make up some instructions of their own to follow. The number of instructions should be increased depending on the age and ability of the children.

■ **Trust me!** Working in pairs, blindfold one of the children. The other then has to help the blindfolded partner get to a designated place by only using verbal instructions (and never helping by physically directing!) This can be developed by sitting the blindfolded partner down at a desk where there are lots of different objects. The other partner has to direct the blindfolded one to carry out certain instructions involving finding, picking up, moving, placing, or doing something else with some of the objects.

■ **Rules.** Instructive language is used for telling people what, or what not, to do. The whole area of rules and their purpose has great potential for discussion. It could be introduced in a general way by just talking about situations in which rules are necessary. How many can the children come up with? Who makes the rules? Why?

■ **Don't do that.** Present children with a scene where children are obviously misbehaving, e.g. throwing food at each other at the dinner table. Ask them to talk about what is happening and then make lists of Do's and Don'ts. Behaviour at a firework display, at a swimming pool make good topics for considering rules.

■ **Rules for others.** A further development of this is to get children to think up rules for specific categories of people or animals, e.g. rules for babies, teachers, parents, cats, teenagers, librarians, etc.

Rules tend to be written in negatives - don't do this or that. Look at the school Code of Conduct on this page. The language is all positive. Get the children to think back to some of the activities they have done and to revise their sets of rules so that they are all positive!

■ This work on rules could easily lead on to producing posters and notices displaying some of the rules.

1. Look after the school buildings and environment - we want it to stay looking nice.
2. Take a pride in how you look and how you present your work.
3. Think of your own and other people's safety in and around school.
4. Take care of other people's belongings wherever they may be.
5. There are times for noise and times for quietness.
6. Be polite and well-mannered to everyone.
7. Try not to talk when others are - listen to what other people have to say.
8. Be friendly towards visitors and new children.
9. Treat other people as you would like to be treated.
10. Remember to smile!

DIRECTING

We often need to use instructive language when we are giving other people directions on how to get to different places.

- Children need to be able to explain things in a logical and orderly way.
- They should be able to structure and sequence the information in order to make it easily understandable to the listener.

Giving instructions or directions is very much concerned with being able to explain or organise your thinking in a logical and coherent way. It often concerns ordering directions or chunks of information in as simple and understandable a sequence as possible, e.g. first you do this, then that. Finally, you do so-and-so ..., etc.

It is often concerned with explaining or telling people how to get to certain places. For the giver of instructions this may involve identifying landmarks clearly, clarity of direction and conciseness. Sometimes it may be with reference to plans or maps.

Another form of directive language is actually being able to give instructions on how to get a job done or helping someone understand something more clearly. This means identifying and sequencing the various processes involved. In a sense this is what effective teaching is all about!

Directing other people. Begin by working within the classroom environment where the children can use visual cues to support their language. In pairs ask them to make up questions for each other like 'How would you get from the door to the library corner?'. They have to take it in turns to ask and answer, and comment on the accuracy of the partner's instructions. Then make it more difficult by getting them to describe how to get to certain places within the school. You could give them a list, e.g. How would you get from the Head's office to the hall? or they could make up their own questions for each other. Instructions could be recorded on a cassette and then actually used and followed to see how accurate they were.

■ **In the neighbourhood.** The same idea could be used for going places in the locality. Children could be asked to program the robot to get to school from their home or to move about to other places in the locality.

■ **Using maps and plans.** All the above activities could be supported by providing simple maps or plans to refer to. A step forward from this is to provide maps or plans, of an appropriate level of difficulty, and asking the children to use them to give instructions on getting from place to place in less well-known environments.

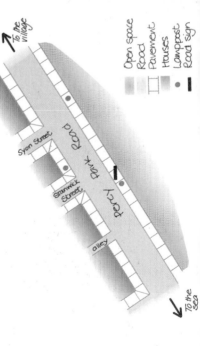

To the village
Syon Street
Stanwick Street
Ronald Road
Percy Park
alley
To the sea

Open space
Road
Pavement
Houses
Lamppost
Road sign

Directing a robot. Ask the children to imagine they have a robot who can help them do lots of jobs, but will only do exactly what you tell it to do. You have to be careful to think of all the instructions and not miss out any steps. Break all the tasks down into smaller tasks to make them perfectly understandable.

■ **Tidy-up time.** Look at the picture of Jitendra's room. What instructions would you give it for tidying up this room? Work out your instructions with a friend. Remember, that you have to give the robot specific instructions. Get together with another pair and explain your robot's instructions to them. Ask them to tell you if you missed anything out.

Jobs around the house. Give the children a set of pictures showing something being done in stages, e.g. making a sandwich, mending a puncture, washing your hair. In pairs ask the children to sequence the pictures in the correct order. Next get them to work out a set of instructions to go with the pictures that would be good enough to give to the robot. Ask groups to compare sets of instructions to see if any stages have been left out. To make this more difficult give out the set of pictures with some stages missing, or just tell the groups what you want them to explain without giving any supporting pictures.

■ *Playing games.* Imagine you were trying to program your robot to play simple games, e.g. noughts and crosses, conkers, hangman, draughts, etc. Discuss together exactly what you would need to tell it to do. Think about what it would need, what the idea of the game is, the order in which things need to be done, etc.

ASKING QUESTIONS TO DEDUCE A SPECIFIC ANSWER

When we want or need to know something one way of finding out is by asking questions.

Who did it?

Where did you see it?

How did it work?

When did it take place?

Why did it happen?

What was it in?

- This involves the ability to adopt a flexible approach to asking questions, usually beginning with trial and error, but then, by remembering what has gone before, eliminating possible options and by making deductions based on the accumulating evidence, to refine and focus questions in a more systematic way.

There is a great deal of skill in asking questions. Among other things it involves:

- how we ask or the way in which we ask
- who we ask; are we asking the best/right person?
- what we ask; are we clear about what we want to know?
- are we asking the right sort of questions?

Obviously asking a question is usually followed by someone responding in some way. Questioning therefore has close links with things like instructing, explaining, informing or describing.

What am I thinking of? Collect a set of 20 or so pictures of animals, forms of transport, people, etc. One partner chooses an animal, for example, without telling the other. Partner 2 then has to ask questions to try and discover which one has been chosen and to eliminate others, e.g. has it got two legs? Partner 1 is only allowed to say yes or no. The idea is to see who can win by using the least number of questions.

Themes could be supplied to help create some parameters to choose within, e.g. a place I like to visit, tools, things that I see on my way to school, someone from the entertainment world, someone from history, etc. Partner 2 then has to ask questions to identify who or what has been chosen.

■ **The 'Why' game.** Almost from the time we begin to talk we want to know why this or why that! Asking 'why?' is the basis of a challenging and competitive game which is great fun.

Partner 1 is only allowed to ask 'why?'. The other partner has to keep thinking of appropriate answers for as long as possible. Give the children a picture and a question to get them going, e.g. This boy is diving off dangerously high cliffs. Why? Because he has seen someone in difficulty in the sea. Why? Because the girl was swimming and got too tired. Why? Because the tide was too strong. Why? Because the girl was swimming and got too tired. Why? ...

How many answers can Partner 2 give before drying up?

You may have to set a time limit or you could be playing this all day!

YES

FRAMING THE RIGHT QUESTIONS

- Framing the right questions requires good preparation and planning.
- It means thinking ahead and anticipating.
- It involves making judgements and inferences.

Framing questions in advance of an activity helps you focus your thinking and makes the activity more purposeful.

Framing the right questions is a way of getting the most out of an experience or activity. It involves you in thinking through what sort of information or outcome you would like. It often involves being able to anticipate and think ahead. It means making value judgements and asking questions like:

- What sort of information am I interested in?
- What would I like to know about?
- What am I likely/unlikely to find out by doing ...?
- What do I already know about this?
- What else do I need to know?
- What sort of information is important?

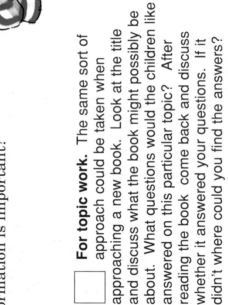

For visitors. Planning and preparation before a visitor comes to talk to the class can make such a visit so much more productive. Whenever you have visitors in to school to talk about particular topics discuss their visits beforehand with the class. Ask them to imagine what sort of things they think the visitor might talk about. What sort of things would they like the visitor to talk about? Brainstorm ideas and begin to draw up areas that the children wish to know more about. Get children to frame certain questions they would like to have answered should they not be raised.

For topic work. The same sort of approach could be taken when approaching a new book. Look at the title and discuss what the book might possibly be about. What questions would the children like answered on this particular topic? After reading the book come back and discuss whether it answered your questions. If it didn't where could you find the answers?

For surveys. Framing questions for surveys, carrying them out, collating the results and then analysing the data, making deductions from it and reporting your findings to others involves a whole range of important language skills, including questioning. Children could carry out class surveys on hobbies, favourite things, etc.

Some questions I would like to ask if only I could!

Sometimes we see things that we would like to know more about - but may never be able to! Sometimes we have to be satisfied with questions left unanswered.

■ Give children a picture to look at. It could be a straightforward scene (usually best if there are plenty of things going on in it) or it could be of a person or just one object. Give the same picture to several groups and ask them to come up with as many questions as they can about the picture that they would like answered. Explain that the questions can be as original as they like! Get the different groups to share their thoughts. It's surprising the variety of unexpected responses you get!

A

■ As a follow-up it is good to encourage the groups to think up imaginative answers to the questions.

■ **Looking at a series of pictures.** This activity can also be extended to series of pictures which might tell part or all of a story. What don't the pictures tell that the children might want to know?

■ **What happened?** Using pictures like the one in **A**, it is possible to generate a lot of questioning language, e.g. Do you think anyone was hurt? Why? What do you think the policeman and the driver are saying? How do you think the owner of the shop is feeling? What is the woman with the pram saying?, etc.

Imaginative questions. Another imaginative approach is to present groups with different scenarios, e.g. Supposing you were able to interview an alien from another planet, or a famous character from history, what would you want to know? What would you ask them?

■ *Suggest that each group brainstorms and comes up with as many suggestions as possible. (It might be a good idea to note them down.)*

■ *After this, get them to look critically at their list and refine it to what they think are the best, say, five or ten questions. Different groups could then compare responses and discuss the results.*

■ *Perhaps this could be developed into some role-playing where different children take on the part of the interviewer and the interviewee, and have fun making up possible answers!*

USING QUESTIONS IN PROBLEM-SOLVING

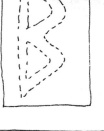
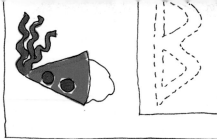

The following are examples of a fairly open-ended approach which requires some imagination, some planning and an ability to see things from other people's perspectives.

In everyday life we are forever being presented with problems that need resolving. Sometimes they may be fairly immediate, sometimes we may have more of an opportunity to plan or think longer-term about them.

Often, we need to use language to help resolve things by articulating the problem, by sharing with others, explaining it to others, or by asking questions to help understand or clarify it.

Choosing a new school. Imagine you were moving to a new town and had the choice of two schools. What would you, as a pupil, want to know about each one to help you make your choice? What would your parents want to know? Would it be different?

■ **A class visit.** Imagine you are going on a class visit. You could suggest a place to the group or allow them to decide. You need to inform all parents of the arrangements. What would you need to tell them? (Ask groups to compare answers! This should prove very interesting!) This activity could easily lead on to getting them to draft out the letter too.

- The skilful use of questioning is important in helping to resolve problems or to plan effectively.
- Deciding what sort of information you want or someone else might want to know helps you structure your questions better.

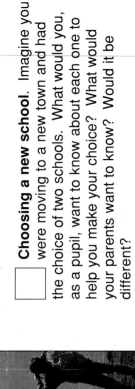

■ **Planning a party.** Your parents say you can have a party. There are all sorts of decisions and plans to be made. Brainstorm and list all that needs considering and doing.

■ This work can extend far beyond just speaking and listening work. Invitations, hats and masks can be designed and made. Cakes can be baked, sandwiches and fillings produced. The organisation and planning skills are the ones being developed here.

■ **A police interview.** The police come to interview you. If you were the policeman or woman what questions would you want to ask? Your bike is stolen.

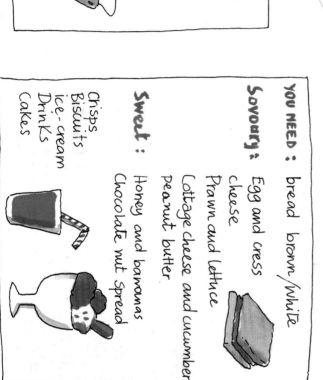

Colour mask

cut paper into strips

board

INVITATION

TWO TYPES OF INVITATIONS

JOHN INVITES LINDA TO HIS BIRTHDAY PARTY

Come to my Party! John

YOU NEED : bread brown/white

Savoury: Egg and cress cheese
Prawn and lettuce
Cottage cheese and cucumber
Peanut butter

Sweet : Honey and bananas
Chocolate nut spread

Chisps
Biscuits
ice-cream
Drinks
Cakes

☐ *Asking questions to help structure the learning for others.* This is basically what lies at the heart of most of the questions asked in the classroom. It involves deciding what it is that you consider important and worth learning and structuring your questions to enable the learner to focus on these points.

- Read a variety of appropriate shortish texts with a group which are designed to be used for fairly straightforward comprehension purposes and have a mixture of questions after the text, e.g. of a literal, inferential, evaluative nature, etc.

- Do the activity orally but as each question is asked and answered get the children to consider why the question was asked, what its purpose was, and draw their attention to the variety and form of questions.

- When they have had some experience at this provide them with a similar text and ask them to make up their own set of questions for others to answer.

- To make the activity even more meaningful the children could swap those of others and have a go at answering questions and actually marking their friends' work too!

INTERVIEWING

Asking the right sort of questions gives you a better chance of eliciting the right sort of information.

Sometimes questions may arise quite spontaneously and naturally during the course of events; sometimes they may be anticipated or planned in advance.

Interviewing others offers a more planned approach to using questioning language. Getting the most out of interviewing people requires some form of advance planning and anticipation, e.g. where? when? how? why? what? who?

- The interview situation provides a more structured and directed approach towards identified desired outcomes.
- It enables you to consider in some detail what sort of things you would like to know, so that appropriate questions might be framed in advance.
- It is a good way of making the most out of visits, e.g. when studying a neighbourhood.
- It is a good way of preparing for, and making the most of, visitors to the school, e.g. an old person talking about his or her childhood, the visit of a policeman, etc.
- It is an important skill in carrying out surveys effectively.

> Where? when? how? why? what? who?

Interviewing one another in the class. Carry out a survey of children's interests, hobbies, leisure time activities or interesting places they may have visited. Produce a class list (with due sensitivity to children who may be embarrassed by lack of response in some categories).

- Each child could then pick another child (or two) in the class to interview, ensuring that all children are selected at least once. Talk together first about the sorts of questions that could be asked in order to find out more information from each other. Give the children a little time to prepare their questions before interviewing anyone.
- The results of the interviews could be written up as a 'Guess who?' article for the wall so everyone can learn a little more about others in their own class.

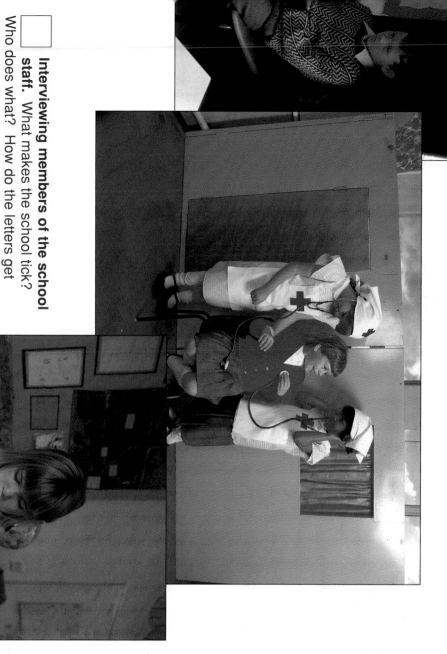

Interviewing members of the school staff. What makes the school tick?

Who does what? How do the letters get typed? Who opens and cleans the school? There are lots of interesting things to be discovered right on your own doorstep! How many different people contribute towards the running of your school? Have a brainstorming session and list as many as you can together.

■ Check first that individual members of staff have no objection to being interviewed! Explain that the groups will have the opportunity to interview a member of staff and tape record it for others to hear.

■ Ask groups of children to select a particular member of staff and discuss what questions they would like to ask (of a non-embarrassing nature!) You may wish to give some guidance beforehand.

■ Get the groups to write down their questions. When they feel they have finished suggest they look at the list and reduce it to what they consider to be the three or four most interesting questions.

■ Get the group to write a short introduction to the person being interviewed which can be read onto the tape just before the interview. Make sure that each child will have a chance to ask a question and that the group has planned and arranged what to say and each child knows their part.

■ Record the interviews and have fun playing them to others. What did groups think of other's attempts? The interviews could be written up as a Staff Profile.

Interviewing people in the neighbourhood. *The same sort of approach could be taken to interviewing people from the locality, e.g. in relation to a local study, etc.*

CLASSIFYING AND CATEGORISING

Comparative Language involves the ability to compare different things, ideas and opinions in order to make judgments based on their merits or meanings. We are constantly classifying and categorising things either consciously or unconsciously. This is necessary in order to cope with life and to help us learn. Sometimes our survival may depend on it. Classifying and categorising involves making comparisons and discerning similarities and differences, e.g. a cat and a dog both have four legs and a tail, a cat goes miaow but a dog barks.

- Often things will have similar attributes but will also be different in many ways.
- We make decisions based on our existing knowledge.

Tastes nice

Tastes nasty

Comparative language is involved in decision-making. It is often used to enable us to weigh up situations in order to make a decision, e.g. you only have enough money to buy either a bar of chocolate or a bag of boiled sweets - chocolate is nicer but it goes too quickly; you get more boiled sweets to share; they last longer.

The language we use is likely to be influenced by our own past experiences and knowledge, by our own personal preferences, attitudes, tastes and opinions.

When using comparative language we may simply reinforce our existing attitudes or our behaviour may be influenced by others and be changed. Consider the voice of the politician, 'Look at what a mess they have got us in over the last five years. Now if you voted for me my party would ...'

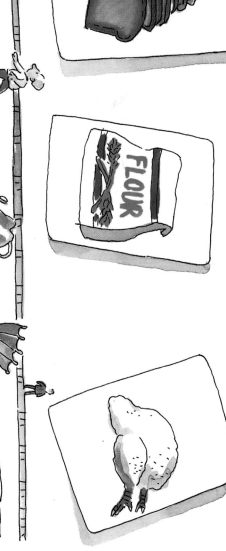

The Food Game. Provide the children with a set of about 15-20 different pictures of food.

■ Ask the children to sort the foods into different groups, e.g. foods that should be eaten hot, food that you buy frozen, food that is in liquid form, food that is 'foreign', food that you eat as a dessert, etc. Children must explain to each other their choices.

■ Working together, get the children to pick pairs of cards and explain the reasons for their choices using the following pattern, e.g. the hamburger is the same as the sausage because they both contain meat.

■ True or not true. Each child picks a food picture and makes a statement about it. The other child/ren have to decide whether it is true or not, e.g. the bread contains flour, apple pie is eaten with a straw. True or not true?

■ This game could be played with different types of animals, transport, people's faces, etc.

☐ **Safe or dangerous?** Compare a range of everyday household objects and decide under what conditions they may be considered safe or dangerous, e.g. toothpaste, a penknife, a bottle of aspirin, a packet of crisps, etc.

■ **Silly or sensible?** Provide the children with a picture of a scene which has a number of 'silly' things in it, e.g. a wheelbarrow with square wheels, a policeman standing on his head, etc. The children have to discuss and decide what is 'normal' and what is 'absurd'. The children could have fun by drawing their own pictures for their friends to discuss.

DECISION-MAKING

In this unit we see the use of comparative language in comparing and contrasting two slightly different pictures. Children use the information gained as a basis for making a decision and supporting it. We are encouraging the skill of looking carefully.

- Children can learn about comparative language by:
  - looking carefully and describing accurately the differences in two contrasting pictures
  - expressing opinions as a result of considering the pictures
  - considering why others' opinions might be different from yours.

☐ **Inspector Factfinder.** Provide the children with two pictures of a room - a 'before' and 'after-the-robbery' picture. The children have to be Inspector Factfinder and have to identify clues in the second picture that tell that a robbery has taken place.

■ **Changes in fashion.** Provide the children with two photographs/drawings, one showing a child or adult dressed in style prevalent at turn of century, one of present day. Ask children to describe each picture and say what they like about each. Then discuss in what way fashions have changed and how the pictures are different. Ask them which style they prefer and why.

■ **In the past.** Provide the children with maps or photos of areas as they were some time ago and as they are today. Ask children to compare and discuss observable changes.

■ **Comparing pictures.** Provide photos or pictures of two very contrasting or different landscapes, buildings, works of art, etc. Ask children to discuss in what ways they are different. Ask them to compare the pictures and explain their own personal preferences.

Going on Holiday. In decision-making we may have a range of options to choose from. We need to consider the the merits of each before making decisions.

■ You are going on holiday to a hot country for a fortnight. You are going to stay in a hotel near the sea. On this page are some of the things you might need to take.

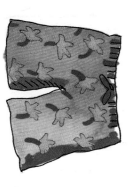

swimming costume

money

T-shirt

air ticket

passport

JOHN SMITH

shorts

suntan lotion

a book to read

■ Make a list together of all the things you will need to take. You might like to divide it into 'things to wear' and 'other things'.

■ When you have made your list, look at it again with a partner. Unfortunately you are only allowed to take a limited amount of luggage. You are only allowed to take ten items of clothing and six other things.

■ Discuss what you should take and what you should leave. Make a final list.

■ When you have finished compare your list with another group's. Are they very different? Why? Who has the best list?

IMPLICATIONS

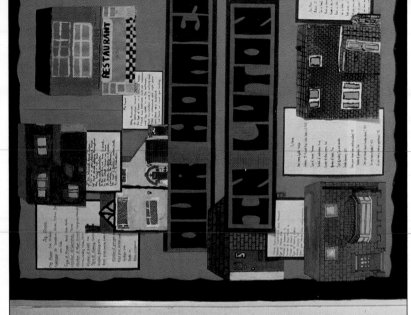

It is interesting for children to compare their present environment, e.g. classroom, school, playground, home, area, town, with a view of how they would like things to be.

- What are the implications of your thinking?
- This unit requires children to think about some of the practicalities and difficulties of effecting change.

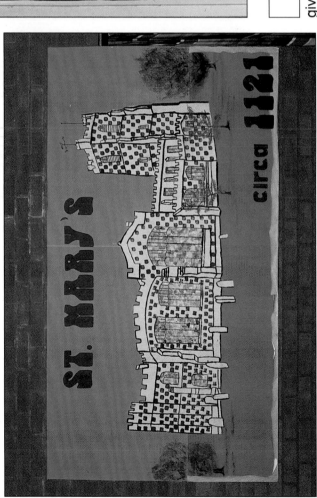

This type of language usage lends itself to weighing evidence, considering other people's points of view on any subject. It would be possible to consider any topic, e.g. boys are stronger than girls, or the value of advertising, and consider the pros and cons.

Luton's looking up! The people of Luton recently decided it was time to give their town a better image by making improvements to the way the town looked. First of all they considered what was wrong with the town. They looked at things, asked questions and made lists.

■ They then considered what could be done. Some things could be done fairly quickly, e.g. putting strong, attractive litter bins in places where people threw litter; decorating roundabouts in the middle of roads; putting baskets of flowers on railings.

■ Some things took longer, e.g. improving the efficiency of the bus services; publicising the campaign by encouraging everyone to help - by getting into schools to talk to children and explaining what they were doing, by articles in the newspapers, etc.

■ Children could share out the roles and develop this work as a simulation.

■ Consider your classroom or your playground. What would you like to see changed? What is wrong with it now? Make a list with a partner. Compare your list with another group's.

■ What do the changes you would like to see involve? Do they involve money? Could any improvements be made without spending any money? Are your suggestions realistic?

■ All improvements mean that someone has to do something. Who would carry out the improvements? Who would give their time to do the work? Are there any little things that could be done straight away that would help?

■ How could you get others involved? How would you let other children know what you were considering? What other things would you need to think about?

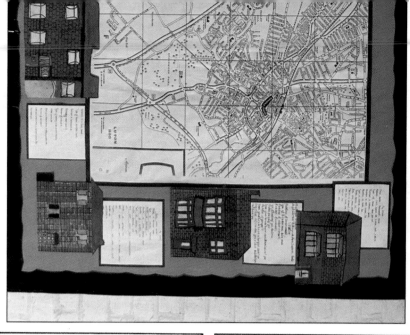

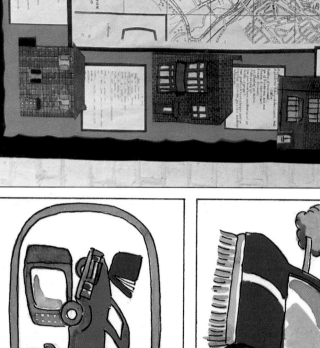

☐ *'If I ruled the world'.* Ask children to write or discuss their ideas and compare them with each other. Through discussion, get them to cut the list down to 3 or 4 possibilities. The same sort of thing is possible with the 'I wish I could ...' idea.

■ *Invent a machine.* You invent a machine that can do the housework. Which jobs would you want it to do? Compare lists and refine them to just five choices.

■ *The time capsule.* You are burying a time capsule which is to hold five things that will tell future generations about our present-day world. Which five objects will you enclose?

■ *The desert island.* You are being cast away on a desert island. Which ten things will you take to help you survive? Compare lists.

■ *Favourite TV programmes.* Write down your favourite five TV programmes. Discuss them with a partner. Justify your choices. Compare them with another group's. Produce a combined 'Top Five TV Programmes' List. Compare this with another group's.

■ *Comparing literature.* Have prepared, or read, two or three different openings to stories. They could be from stories by famous authors, e.g. the beginning to The Iron Man by Ted Hughes, or pieces written by children in the class. Compare them. Talk about authors' different styles. Ask what the children liked about each. Discuss how effective they were.

BUILDING ON CHILDREN'S EXPERIENCES

Imaginative language is the ability to translate mental images into words and convey them to others.

- Imagination involves the ability to form mental images of:
  - objects
  - situations or events or people not actually present.
- It involves:
  - empathy
  - conjecture
  - a willingness to be adventurous and play with images
  - creativity
  - resourcefulness.
- Problem-solving requires a degree of imagination.

There is often a tendency to toss children in at the deep end without any waterwings! Many children need a lot of support when being encouraged to use imaginative talk.

Activities in this unit are examples based on experiences which are within the realm of children's own possible experiences. Encourage the children to relate these situations to their own experiences and use anecdotal talk to personalise them.

The parcel. Get the children to consider pictures and questions like the ones in **A**.

■ Now the children can talk about which of these they liked best. Can they think of a better ending for this story?

A

Who do you think this girl is? Why is she looking out of the window? What is she thinking?

How has the expression on the girl's face changed? How do you think she is feeling? Why do you think she feels excited?

Who do you think the parcel is for?

Every person has a story to tell! For this you will need half a dozen photographs or drawings of different people.

■ Do you ever see people in your town and around your street or wonder who they are? They all have different lives, with different likes and dislikes. Look at the pictures.

■ Have fun making up names for each of the people. Make up some facts about each one, e.g. What do they do? Where do they live? What sort of music do they like?, etc. There are lots of things you can make up about them.

■ Try to make up a story about one or two of them. Imagine they are ...

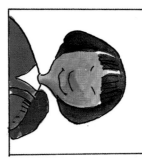

Name

Address

Occupation

Likes

Dislikes

Putting yourself in someone else's shoes. Encouraging children to put themselves in someone else's place is a way of stimulating their imagination. It is good to begin with people they know, e.g. their parents, brothers or sisters, friends, a teacher, etc. Ask them to discuss questions like:

- *What do you think ... would say in such and such a situation?*
- *How would he or she react?*
- *What would they be feeling?*
- *What do you imagine they think about such and such?, etc.*

If you ask groups to think about the same person, e.g. a teacher, different groups' responses could be compared.

■ You could develop this by asking them how people in particular jobs would respond or behave in particular circumstances, e.g. a policeman, an explorer, etc. This has very close links with predictive language. Pictures of different people, of different ages, in different situations are good for encouraging children to project and empathise too.

PROBLEM-SOLVING

● Encourage children to speculate and make hypotheses, and to use exploratory language.

Problem-solving in collaborative group situations is a good way of eliciting imaginative talk. The following are some examples of this approach.

Moral dilemmas like this are plentiful in school life! Bullying, lying, cheating, copying, being unkind, etc., are all possibilities for themes to explore.

A moral dilemma. Pose a story problem like the one here.

At breaktime Ian goes back to his classroom to get his ball. Just as he is about to go in he sees Wesley looking in Sarah's desk. The bell goes and so Ian goes straight in. Wesley looks up and blushes. When everyone is back in the classroom Sarah bursts into tears. Her new set of pencils has gone missing. What should Ian do?

■ Talk about these possible courses of action with a partner. Try to decide which is the best. Try to list the possibilities in order.

- Should he keep quiet and ask Wesley about it later?
- Should he say nothing at all?
- Should he ask Wesley if he can borrow some of his felt tips and watch how he reacts?
- Should he tell the teacher or Sarah what he saw?
- Should he offer to give Sarah his felt tips?
- Something else?

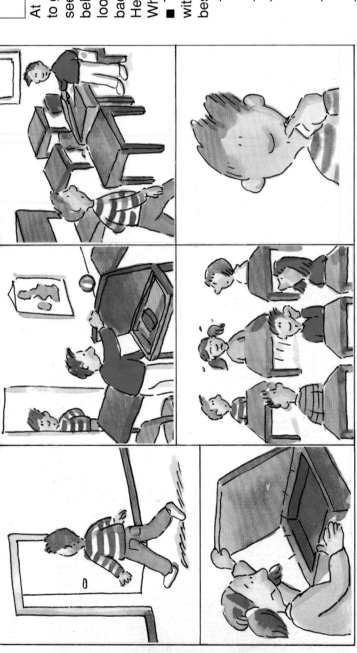

Mission impossible! Your task - to get a friend out of enemy jail. Your friend is in a jail guarded by a huge and tough jailer. The keys to unlock the jail are on a ring on his belt. To get to the jail you have to swim across a shark-infested river. You also have to pass through a wood where vicious wolves roam. In front of the jail is a tall electric fence. Discuss and work out a plan of action with a partner. Compare your solution with another group's. Discuss whose ideas have the most chance of succeeding.

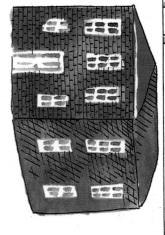

How many different uses ... A brick is used for building ... but it can also be used for a book-end, for standing on, for throwing through a jeweller's shop window, etc.

■ Talk about how many different uses you and a partner can come up with. Get together with another group and share your ideas.

■ The 'how many uses can you think of for a ...' idea is a fruitful and inexhaustible avenue to explore, e.g. a paper clip, a drawing pin, a lollipop stick, etc.

Beginnings and endings. Another variation of this is to give each group a sentence beginning, e.g. The curly-haired girl opened the window and ... How many different endings are possible?

■ *What if ...? questions.* A similar idea for generating imaginative language is to ask some 'What would you do if ...?' questions, e.g.
- *What if the sun shone for 24 hours every day?*
- *What if you couldn't stop hiccupping for an hour?*
- *What would you change if you ruled the world?*

THE REALMS OF FANTASY

This leads us into the realms of fantasy where there are virtually no ground rules. The only limits are really the extent of the children's imaginations! The possibilities are endless. These examples are just a few starters!

- The stimulus for generating this sort of talk often comes from reading to the children and talking about what has been read, or looking at a picture stimulus or from something they have seen on TV or heard about.
- Some children will need more structure and support than others.
- Encourage a fearless, adventurous, never-mind-if-it's-impossible type of language.
- Working together with friends who are trusting and accepting is the most supportive context for these activities!

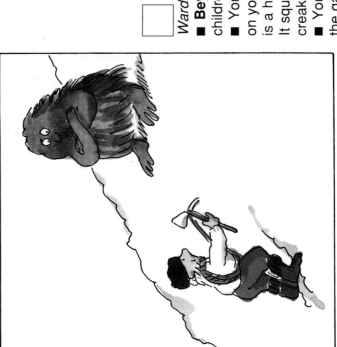

Read and discuss favourite fantasy stories such as *Tom's Midnight Garden*, *The Hobbit* or *The Lion, The Witch and The Wardrobe*. Mysterious narrative poems like *Flannan Isle* are useful.

- **Beyond the door.** Set the scene by providing a context the ask the children to get together in pairs and imagine what happens next.
- You are out in the countryside and are walking through the woods on your own. You come across an old, crumbling, high brick wall. In it is a heavy wooden gate with an old rusty bolt. You pull the bolt back. It squeals with protest. You push hard against the door and it slowly creaks open ...
- Your heart is pounding as you race down the alleyway to escape the gang of older children who are chasing you. There is no way out! Suddenly you see a dingy doorway with a door half-open. It's your only chance ...

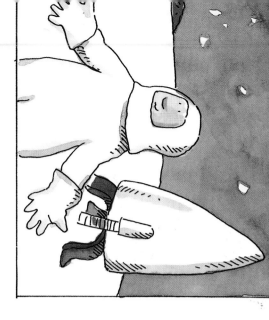

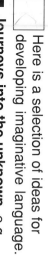

Here is a selection of ideas for developing imaginative language.

■ **Journeys into the unknown**, e.g.
- exploring unknown planets
- exploring uncharted jungles
- journeys to desert islands
- journeys under the sea (Jules Verne).

■ **Adventure ideas**, e.g.
- human endeavour (climbing the Himalayas, meeting the Yeti)
- lost treasure
- hidden cities and historical exploration (the lost tribes of the Incas, tomb robbers, etc.)
- strange lands.

■ **Mysterious events**, e.g.
- unsolved crimes
- mysterious disappearances
- the appearance of mysterious creatures or beings.

■ **Animal themes**, e.g.
- unusual and wild animals
- prehistoric or imaginary animals.

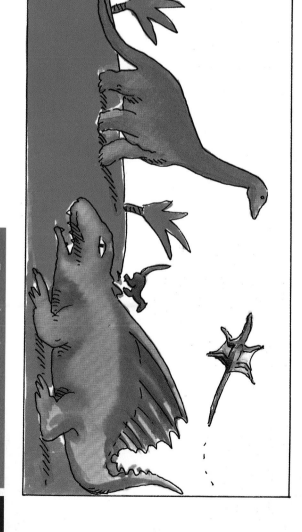

The future. The future is a good topic for imaginative talk because who is to say what will be possible or impossible?

■ *Dreams.* The idea of dreams is a good way in and links nicely with the last idea, e.g. You have a dream several times and in that dream you picture a sliding door which leads you into another world, in another age. To your great surprise, when you visit an old uncle you see exactly this same door in one of the upstairs rooms. Dare you slide it back?

■ *In a hundred years.* What will the world be like in 100 years from now? What changes will there be in your home? in school? in transport?, etc. This topic makes possible the whole idea of creating imaginary beings from other planets, or as yet unthought of inventions for the home, etc.

CAN YOU GUESS ...?

Can guess what this unit is going to be about? Our lives are routine, patterned and predictable in many ways. When we press a switch a light comes on. When we get up we clean our teeth. Night follows day. This patterning helps us to cope. We learn to expect things to happen or behave in a particular sequence or way. It is the same with language. It does not occur in a vacuum. Language itself has a certain predictability and we often use it to help us predict what might happen or how people might act or speak.

- Predictability is important in the patterning of language.
- It helps limit the range of possibilities and enables us to make informed guesses about what people might say (or write).
- The context or situation gives us clues as to what sort of language may appropriately be used or what might be said.
- When predicting what people might say or do we are helped by knowing what has happened previously and our understanding of the way things tend to happen.
- Sometimes the way people look or act can give us clues as to what they might say.
- Language itself has its own structure and predictable patterns which limit the possible range of words that can be used in particular ways and situations.

Can you guess what each of these might be saying?

The situation, or the context, in which language takes place helps us to predict the sorts of things that might be said and the way in which they might be said.

We speak differently to different sorts of people in different situations.

Sometimes the way people look and act help us to predict what they might say.

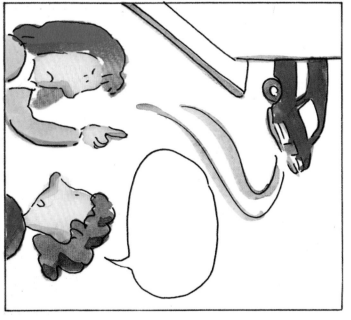

Children speak differently to their friends in the playground than to their teachers in the classroom.

We would probably speak differently to the plumber than to the Prime Minister.

We would speak differently in a public meeting than we would at home.

Can you predict what these people are about to say?

Predicting story endings. How do you think this story will end? Amir and Nishat were walking through the woods. Nishat saw some footprints. They led to a wooden chest that was hidden in some bushes.

- Our knowledge of the way stories are written and told, our knowledge of the way things tend to happen and our understanding of the context in which things happen all help predictability.

- Our knowledge of language structure itself limits the range of words we use in given situations and therefore helps us to predict what people might say.

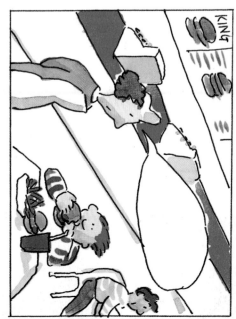

The language we use and understand depends on our life experiences and knowledge of language itself. This is why as educators we seek to provide a broad range of worthwhile experiences and to help children learn more about how language works.

SPEAKING WITHOUT TALKING!

Sometimes we can predict what people might say by the way they look or act, or by the things they do. We often use non-verbal cues and children must realise their importance.

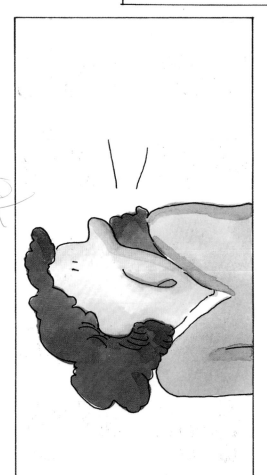

■ Ask children how they knew what to do, what sort of mood they thought you were in, etc.

■ Pursue this line of discussion by asking things like how people can tell whether someone is happy, sad, excited, etc.

■ How do people know when you don't want to talk to them? When you are fed up? What are the tell-tale signs?

■ This can be followed up by some role playing where you ask children to act out feeling excited, sad, etc. Some children could make up mimes whilst the others guessed what feelings the actors were portraying.

Look - no words! To introduce the idea that we can speak without talking. This can be a teacher-led whole class discussion.

■ Introduce the idea by indicating with your hands only that you want the children to stand, to sit, that you want one child (indicate by pointing at them) to come out the front (indicate by beckoning them), etc. Look angry.

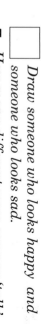

Looking at pictures. Children could look at pictures similar to those that appear on this page. Talk about:

- How do you think each of these people feel?
- What clues are there?
- What do you think might have happened to make each one feel like that?
- What might each person be saying?
- What would you say to each one?

Draw someone who looks happy and someone who looks sad.

■ *How many different ways can you 'talk' with your hands? Act some of them out!*

■ *Can you use these signals to talk to a friend?*

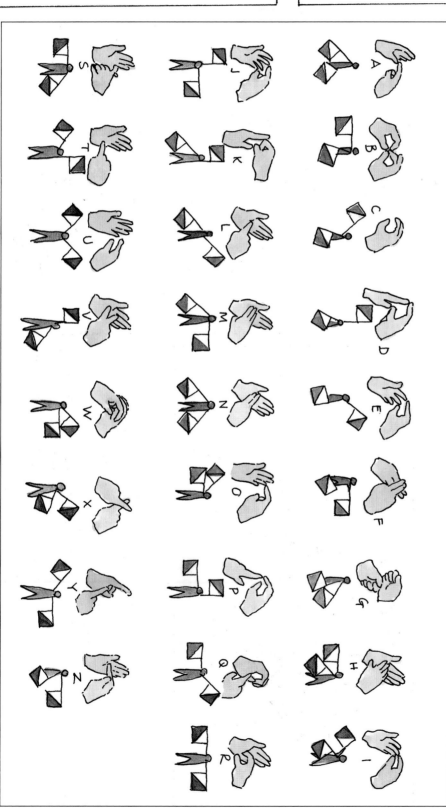

THE THINGS PEOPLE SAY

- We tend to talk to different people, e.g. our friends, the Head Teacher, a doctor, in different ways.
- The situation, or context, in which we are speaking affects what we say and how we speak.

Sometimes the jobs people do or the roles they are playing make it easier to predict the sorts of things they are likely to say, e.g. doctors in their surgery have a certain way of speaking to people, policemen or women on duty tend to speak in a certain way too. We all have certain 'favourite' things we say in certain situations.

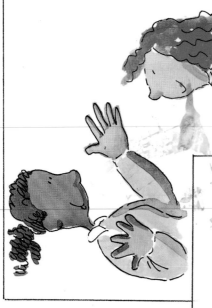

What sort of things ... In small mixed groups of 2-4, children can discuss pictures like the ones in this unit together.

Introduce this unit by asking things like:

- Do you talk differently to your friends on the playground than you would talk to me in the classroom? (Try to tease out in what ways.)
- Do you talk differently to the parents of a friend that you don't know very well, than you would to your own parents? Why? In what ways?
- Do your parents talk differently to you when you have a special visitor?
- Would you expect a postman to talk differently from the Prime Minister? Why? In what ways?
- Do people's jobs affect the way they talk and the sorts of things they might say?
- What sort of things would you expect a ... to say or to talk about?
- Do you talk differently on the telephone?

■ **Teachers.** What sorts of things would your teacher say when:

- you have done well?
- he or she is cross?
- everyone is talking too much?

■ **Parents.** What sort of things do parents say when:

- it's time for bed?
- they think your bedroom's in a mess?
- they don't like your clothes?
- they want to get you to do things like washing-up, etc?

■ **Friends.** What sort of things do you say to your friends when:

- you fancy some of their crisps?
- you want to join in their game but they won't let you?
- you think something is really good?

■ **Picture talk.** Different people say different sorts of things.

■ Think of between 5 and 10 things each of the people in these pictures might say.

■ Would they speak differently? Act out how you think each one would speak.

▢ *Favourite sayings.* Do different people have favourite sayings?

■ *What are yours? Your parent's? Your teacher's? Your best friend's? Your teacher's?*

■ *What things do people keep saying that really irritate you?*

■ *Carry out a class survey.*

POSSIBILITIES

Given a particular set of circumstances there are a number of things which could happen. Sometimes the range of alternatives will be great. Sometimes the number will be very limited. We predict on the basis of our previous knowledge and present circumstances (and sometimes the limits of our creativity and imagination!).

- When we overhear bits of people's conversations we try to predict what has been said before on the basis of available information, e.g. what we know of the people involved and what we hear - which may sometimes be fairly minimal!

Conversation snippets. Try to predict what the other person might have said when we only hear a snippet of the conversation.

■ You overhear the following bits of someone's telephone conversations.

■ Discuss what you think the people were talking about. Think up as many different and interesting alternatives as possible. When you have finished, share some of your ideas together with other groups!

● Children can role-play some 'bus' conversations overheard, or snippets from the doctor's surgery.

■ It is interesting to discuss how easy it is to jump to the wrong conclusions by hearing only bits of conversations.

... You lost your coat at school?

... You came home all muddy?

... Someone left a three-year-old alone in a house?

... Someone left a jar of sleeping pills lying about?

... There was a power cut for a week?

... The roof blew off of your house?

... The speed limit was reduced to 20 m.p.h?

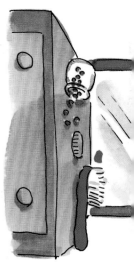

... The world's oil supplies ran out?

... The sun stopped shining?

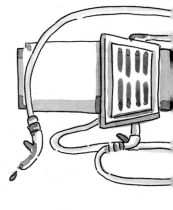

Discuss the range of possible outcomes using the following situations. Some of the situations offer very limited possibilities, others offer more scope. Differentiating these could also be another task for discussion.

■ *Talk about how many different answers children come up with for these questions.*

THE PREDICTABILITY OF LANGUAGE ITSELF

- Sometimes the way our language is structured limits the range of responses that can be predicted and the type of language that can be used.

The very language we speak has a clear structure, underlying logic and pattern. It follows certain rules and conventions which means that it has a degree of in-built predictability. This unconsciously governs how we say things and construct utterances, and means that our intuitive understanding of this underlying framework of language helps us to predict the likelihood of certain things being said in certain ways in various contexts.

Sometimes the range of possibilities can be large. Sometimes the structure of the preceding language will severely limit what can follow. This brings us very much into the realms of language awareness and usage which would take another book itself! We just touch briefly on some aspects of predictability in language structures here.

Predictability in language. Discuss, using these sentences, how some offer a wide range of alternative possibilities whilst others are more limiting. Why is this?
■ Discuss how many different ways you could finish off these sentences:

- Make sure you clean your teeth before ...
- You can't go out unless ...
- We must get to bed early or ...
- Mr Patel could not start his car so ...
- Shireen wore her best dress because ...
- I was angry with my friend because ...
- After tea I am going to ...
- I know how to ...
- One day my dog ...
- My new bike ...
- Yesterday two girls ...

☐ **Phrases.** Explore predictability in phrases, e.g. opposites (big and ...), words that go together (apples and ... knife and ..., etc.).

■ **Rhyming poems.** Look together at examples of rhyming poems - from simple nursery rhymes to more sophisticated poems, and explore the use of language predictability in them.

■ **Rhyme tennis.** For a more fun approach to rhyme, play rhyme tennis. Children can play this in pairs when facing each other. One person 'serves' by saying a word and the other hits the word back by saying a rhyming word. The point is won when children in their pairs cannot think of a rhyme. Limit the game to a list of words for younger children.

☐ *Word association.* The 'tennis' approach can also be used for free association - children responding with the first word that comes into their heads. Interesting combinations can be written down and later drafted into a poem. Talk should develop ideas about connotative meaning and imagary here.

■ **Similes.** Discuss how we often liken something to something else. To do this give some examples of different ways in which different parts of the body can be described, e.g. my hair is like ... fine silk, a hedgehog's back, sticky spaghetti, etc. Ask the children to provide some similes for given parts of the body. In groups, give the children some endings from some similes, e.g. like a squashed tomato, like slimy seaweed, etc. They have to come up with as many possible beginnings to each one as they can.

ᚠᚢᚦᚩᚱ
F U th o R

ᚳᚨᚾᛒ
p S T B

WHAT DOES THAT MEAN?

- We frequently use language:
  - to explore meanings
  - to speculate
  - to make deductions
  - to make inferences.
- Interpretative Language is a way of coming to terms with words or actions that are unclear, ambiguous or unknown in some way.

Interpretative Language has close links with:

✓ **Predictive Language - which is** all to do with making assumptions based on previous experience or knowledge or what is considered possible given the existing evidence.

✓ **Imaginative Language - which is** to do with a willingness to explore possible meanings.

Many stories can have more than one meaning and can be read at different levels

Sometimes the words we say aren't meant to be taken literally, and children should realise that we have to work hard to understand the meaning of spoken or written language. We have to look for clues and make inferences.

Riddles. Riddles are a good way of getting children to use Interpretative Language both in creating, and trying to solve, them. Most children are familiar with the idea of riddles, but it might be a good idea to discuss a few with the whole class first before asking smaller groups to tackle work on them. Discuss their features. Consider the strategies for solving them. Look at the clues and evidence together. Get children to try explain how they solved the riddles.

■ **Types of riddles.** Riddles range from simple to complicated. They can be:

- rhyming riddles, e.g. I am something you have to bake: I'm lovely to eat. I am a ...
- of the 'My first is in hand but not in band' type
- in the form of several straightforward clues, e.g. You can pull me and push me. You can hit me with your fist. You can push things through me. What am I?
- in the form of things described in unusual ways, e.g. I am like a sleepy cow but I roar! I am a bit of a bully because I push things about. Bricks, mud and muck are all the same to me. What am I? (A bulldozer!)

■ Each group can be given a number of appropriate riddles to solve. They should be asked to try to explain and justify their answers and to share their thoughts with other groups.

■ Discussions on the features of riddles could be followed by pairs of children having a try at making up some riddles of their own for other groups to solve. Children could be given a structured way of thinking or could try them without support, e.g. Think of the thing you wish to make a riddle about. Discuss what it actually does and looks like (colour, shape, size, noise, way it moves, what it eats, etc.) Think of what it reminds you of. What is it like? (These things could just be discussed or listed and an appropriate number of clues selected. An extension of this is to number the clues and show them to others one at a time and get them to guess as the evidence accumulates. See who can guess the riddles with the least number of clues!)

X	P	W	+	I
/k	G	W	H	N	I/S

L D A Y

■ **Fables with a moral.** Aesop was a master at telling stories with hidden meanings. They are a rich resource for encouraging children to use interpretative language.

■ To introduce the idea select a well-known fable and read it to the class, e.g. 'The Hare and The Tortoise'. Discuss the story, the setting and the characteristics of the two creatures. Ask what they thought about them. Discuss together what lessons can be learned from the story.

■ In pairs get them to think of one sentence that summarises the essential meaning of the fable. Get them then to make up another story with different characters that has a similar moral.

■ Select other fables to be read together and discussed in a similar way or in smaller groups. Folk tales (like Anansi stories) and cautionary poems (like Matilda poems) are also good for discussing in this way.

■ To extend and follow up children could be given a modern moral, e.g. if you wear wellies with holes in you will get wet feet and asked to make up a story for it.

Proverbs. Proverbs can also be used as a basis for interpretative language. They could be given a list of common proverbs and a list of possible meanings (the correct number, or to make it more difficult, more than needed) and in pairs be asked to match them up and explain why. Alternatively, they could just be given some proverbs and asked to come up with some possible explanations for them.

■ *Runes.* Anglo-Saxon riddles were often written in runes. Use the rune signs to communicate in new ways and even to write authentic-looking riddles for display.

WHERE'S THE EVIDENCE?

Interpretative language is to do with looking for, and recognising, clues which may often be visual or spoken. This often involves using language to eliminate, reason and solve problems.

Visual clues. Have several pictures, a dozen or so, of different characters prepared. One of the group chooses one but does not tell the others who they have selected. The group then have to try to discover which one it is by asking questions, e.g. Is it a man? Only yes/no answers can be given. The group have to work it out by a process of elimination.

■ **'What's my line?'** This can be developed by playing the 'What's my line?' game with a group. 'Twenty questions' is another good old game that requires the use of deduction and interpretative language.

■ **What's it for?** Photos or pictures of unusual objects should be collected and then given to children. They then have to discuss what they think the objects are by looking for clues in the pictures. They should come up with a variety of answers which could be shared and discussed further.

■ **What happened?** Children are given a picture and asked to discuss what they think might just have happened and to offer explanations based on the evidence they can see.

■ **What can you tell about this person?** Give the group a bag with some items in it, e.g. roll-on deodorant, nail polish, a book on cats, some foreign coins, a silk scarf, a dart, etc. The group then have to come up with their guesses as to what sort of a person would own these things and some things they might be able to say about him or her.

■ **The dustbin.** The same idea could be used by giving a list of some things found in a dustbin, or some things dug up by an archaeologist, or some drawings of some unusual objects brought back by spacemen returning from a mission to a strange planet.

Spoken clues.

Hearing half a telephone conversation can be very frustrating but also very intriguing. Do you ever try and work out who the other person is and what they are saying? This scenario is good for stimulating interpretative language.

■ Have various one-sided telephone dialogues written down, e.g. Julie is on the telephone …

Hello, How are you?
Did you really?
What happened?
What did he say?
Oh you didn't, did you?!
Yes that's a good idea. When?
OK See you then. Bye.

Ask the group to decide who is on the other end, why they are ringing and what they are saying. Compare various groups' responses.

Jabberwocky

'Twas brillig, and the slithy toves
Did gyre and gimble in the wabe;
All mimsy were the borogroves,
And the mome raths outgrabe.

'Beware the Jabberwock, my son!
The jaws that bite, the claws that catch!
Beware the Jubjub bird, and shun
The frumious Bandersnatch!'

He took his vorpal sword in hand:
Long time the manxome foe he sought -
So rested he by the Tumtum tree,
And stood awhile in thought.

And as in uffish thought he stood,
The Jabberwock, with eyes of flame,
Came whiffling through the tulgy wood,
And burbled as it came!

One, two! One, two! And through and through
The vorpal blade went snicker-snack!
He left it dead, and with its head
He went galumphing back …

… 'You seem very clever at explaining words, Sir,' said Alice. 'Would you kindly tell me the meaning of the poem called "Jabberwocky"?'
'Let's hear it,' said Humpty Dumpty. 'I can explain all the poems that ever were invented - and a good many that haven't been invented just yet.'

Lewis Carroll

Written clues.

Introduce the idea of 'Jabberwocky' to the class and have fun with discussing the whole area of nonsense words.

■ Follow it up by giving children nonsense words and a range of possible meanings to choose from, e.g.

A boolongo is:
- a kind of Italian meal
- a small drum
- a tiny jungle animal.

Give the children a list of nonsense words and ask them to discuss them and to decide which of the given meaning is best. They must then describe the object and make up a sentence or two using the word in it. Great to share with others! Alternatively they could just be given some nonsense words and make up their own meanings for them. Or you could play 'Call my bluff' together as a class.

■ *Headlines.* Headlines are often tantalisingly ambiguous or give you just enough information to whet your appetite. Prepare a number of headlines yourself, or cut some out of the paper, e.g. 'Cat on a hot tin roof'. The task is for each group to agree on a credible, or incredible, newspaper story to go with each headline.

PERSUASIVE LANGUAGE IN PERSPECTIVE

Language is not just used for imparting information. It is often used to argue a point, to negotiate, to persuade.

✓ Politicians want us to believe they have got all the right answers.

✓ Advertisers want us to buy their products.

✓ Children try to persuade their parents to let them have their way.

✓ Adults persuade children to behave politely especially when visitors come.

✓ Children try to persuade each other to do things they shouldn't.

Persuasive language is used at all levels by all people at different times in different situations.

How do we try to influence people?
What sort of things do we say and do (or not say and do as the case may be!)?
What are our motives?

- Are they good?, e.g. persuading people not to drop litter because we are concerned about pollution.

- Are they bad?, e.g. persuading someone to tell a lie to cover up something you have done wrong?

PERSUASION

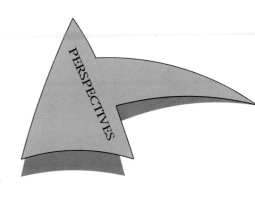

PERSPECTIVES

From point of view of:
- the child
- the parent
- the teacher
- the wider audience, etc.

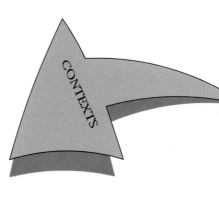

CONTEXTS

- In the home
- In the classroom
- At play
- In the wider world
- In imaginary situations, etc.

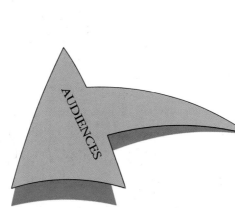

AUDIENCES

- With friends
- With the peer group
- With teachers
- With parents
- With unknown, imaginary audiences, etc.

Effective persuasion often involves:
- Knowing what you want to get or want to happen.
- Wanting to persuade people.
- Having information at your fingertips about your point of view.
- Being able to select information which supports your point of view.
- Knowing what to say that is likely to influence the other person or persons.
- Knowing how to speak in an appropriate way to your audience.
- Being flexible and able to adjust according to the responses from your audience.

Why is it important for children to be able to use and understand persuasive language?

■ To help them understand how best to get across their own point of view, to justify themselves, to argue coherently, etc.

■ To enable them to appreciate some of the issues involved so they can better control situations and not be controlled by them, so they can better realise when they are being persuaded, e.g. by discriminating fact from opinion, to recognise the selective use of information and bias in arguments, etc.

PERSUADING PARENTS

Persuasive language is much in evidence in the home. Parents use persuasive language to try to get children to behave as they want them to, whilst children use persuasive language from an early age to manipulate and get round their parents! In the following activities we consider the use of persuasive language in the context of some typical domestic situations where children want to get something from their parents.

This sequence of activities could be used to help you bring out:

- the importance of having information
- being able to use information selectively to support your position or point of view
- appreciating the appropriateness of context and timing
- sensitivity towards the situation of the target audience.

In a teacher-led discussion with the whole class get children talking about their own pets - their names, type of pets, funny incidents, etc. Encourage anecdotal, personal talk. This activity could easily lead on to doing a class survey on pets.

■ Follow this up using small groups. The composition of the groups could be:

- groups of children who have the same sorts of pets, e.g. those who have dogs
- random groups - ensuring that those children who have no pets at home go in groups where at least one person does.

The idea is to gather information and views from children and to share these with each other in a small group situation. They should be prepared to report these back to the larger group.

■ The children should discuss:
- The good things about having a particular sort of pet.
- What sort of care is needed to look after the pet properly, e.g. training, cleaning, food, etc.
- Expense: of pet, of food, of equipment.
- Disadvantages: time taken up looking after pet, problems of holidays, etc.

Remind children that they will be asked to report back and share their thoughts.

■ After this, using teacher-led and supported whole-class discussion, share the information and views gathered from the small group situations.

■ Ask each group or one member from each group, to report back what they discussed. Ask specific questions to help elicit information.

■ Having gathered together and shared information, you can then move on to a persuasive language task. The objectives for this are to set children a problem to think about and to try and persuade a parent to buy a pet for their child.

■ Mixed groups of 2-4 children are set a problem to think about in the context of a small group. The problem is how could a child persuade her parent to buy him/her a puppy?

■ Outline the following situation to the children. Add or develop or change any of the variables as desired. Discuss the solution to the problem in groups.

Situation: Joanne is 9. She lives in a small three-bedroom semi-detached house in a busy street. She has an elder sister and a younger brother. Joanne's parents both work all day. Joanne badly wants a puppy. How could she persuade her parents to let her have one?

■ Discuss the problem in groups. Give the children as much or as little support as you think necessary.

■ You could give children the following questions to help structure their discussion:

- What do you think Joanne's parents will see as the main difficulties in having a dog?

- What does Joanne need to think carefully about before she asks her parents? Remember all the information gained in the previous activity.

- What sort of things should Joanne say to her parents to help persuade them? Which bits of information would be most advantageous to her cause?

- What things do you think she shouldn't mention? Which things would not help her cause?

- If you were Joanne how do you think she should approach her parents? How should she speak to them? When would be the best time to talk to them?

- How do you think they might respond? What sort of things might they say?

- If Joanne's parents said no, what should she do?

■ Finally, as a class, draw the threads together and help children reflect on their discussions. Bring out the key aspects of persuasive language in action.

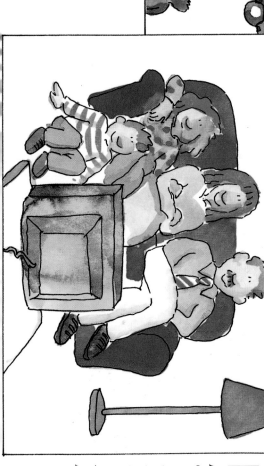

No you can't have a puppy because....

☐ Reflect on the questions from the last group activity bringing out the main points. You could especially bring out the question of selectivity of facts in persuasion. The truth, the whole truth and nothing but the truth? In persuading her parents Joanne may have chosen not to tell them some things, to have left some things unsaid. Is this the same as lying? Is it being honest? Do we all do it at times? Is it right? Does all persuasion involve this?

PERSONAL PROBLEMS AND PERSUASION

Outline the situations below to the children. Add or develop or change any of the variables as desired, e.g. instead of asking them to consider the problem from their perspective ask them to imagine it from an imaginary child's point of view. Discuss the solution to the problem in groups.

Discuss the problems in groups. Give the children as much or as little support as you think necessary. You could provide them with the same sort of structured questions.

☐ Imagine that some of your friends had just been to the Adventure Theme Park an hour's drive away. It **sounds great and you fancy going.** How could you persuade your parents to take you?

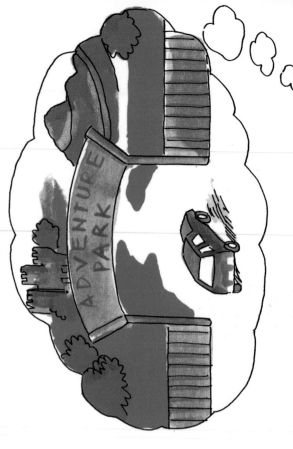

☐ Imagine you want to stay up late to **watch a film on TV.** How do you persuade your parents to let you stay up?

Your best friend has asked you to stay at her house for the weekend.

How could you persuade your parents to let you stay at your friend's house?

FACT FILE

☞ Your parents know your friend and like her. They know her parents too.

☞ Your friend's parents are going out on Saturday night and are going to be late home.

☞ Your parents don't know this.

☞ You have stayed at your friend's house before and there were no problems.

☞ You have some homework to do at the weekend and a test on Monday.

☞ Your aunt is coming to see your parents at the weekend. She hasn't seen you since you were a baby.

While you are out shopping with your Mum you see a pair of the latest Hi Tech trainers in the shoe shop. You can't stop thinking about them. You must have a pair. How can you persuade your parents to let you have the trainers?

FACT FILE

☞ You really want to impress your friends and be the first person to have some.

☞ They are amazingly expensive.

☞ You are very hard on trainers and are always ruining them by getting them muddy or kicking their toes out.

☞ It isn't long since you had your last pair of new trainers.

☞ You have just had a visit from your Gran who gave you £5.

TEMPTATION

We often use language to persuade people to do things that they know they shouldn't by tempting them or even by using persuasive 'threats'. The aim of this unit is to get children to think through some of the issues involved in persuading people to do something wrong or something they may disagree with.

What is it that 'tells us' that something we are being asked to do may be wrong?

Do you always know when you are being asked to do something wrong or something you don't agree with?

Are 'being tempted' and 'being threatened' different?

What sort of people try to persuade you to do or think something wrong? Do your friends? Parents? Teachers? Others? Why?

Do people speak to you differently when they are trying to persuade you to do or think something wrong or that you don't agree with?

What methods do different people use to persuade you in this way?

● Persuasive language can be used for all sorts of purposes, good and bad - it depends on who is doing the persuading and what their motives are.

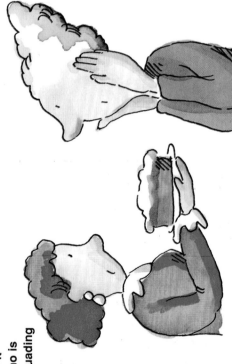

Go on! Have another cream cake.

If you don't do this I won't be your friend!

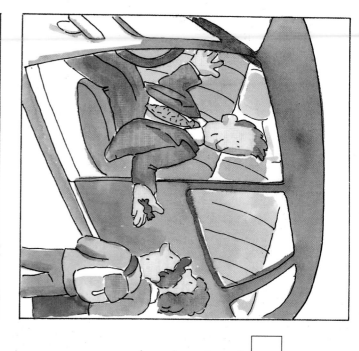

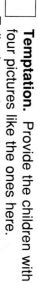

Temptation. Provide the children with four pictures like the ones here.

- Talk about what is happening in each picture.
- What would each of the people be thinking, saying, feeling?
- How will each situation end? Think of several alternatives.
- Have you ever been in any similar situations?

Ask children to discuss situations in which there is a temptation, or in which they personally have been tempted:

- to cheat
- to deceive or tell lies
- to hurt
- to take things that don't belong
- to damage
- to criticise
- to break rules.

PERSUASIVE LANGUAGE IN DECISION-MAKING

• Persuasive language is important in the decision-making process.

Decision-making often involves:

✓ Considering the issues or facts involved in the situation or problem.

✓ Identifying and deciding what you believe, think or feel.

✓ It may mean weighing up the pros and cons fairly dispassionately and choosing the best option or range of options.

✓ It may involve making a snap decision based on your immediate feelings and emotions.

✓ It may mean listening to others' views and modifying your own opinions.

✓ It may mean doing the persuading by supporting and justifying and arguing for your position, by using information and facts selectively to suit your purposes.

✓ The whole process may be more or less influenced by your previous experiences and existing values and beliefs.

The following activities are mostly best approached through discussion in small groups. If appropriate, these may be followed by larger, whole-class discussions giving you the opportunity to reinforce key points and for children to share their thoughts and ideas with a different audience in a different setting.

The idea is to create opportunities for children to discuss and consider different aspects of the use of persuasive language in a range of decision-making situations.

Here are some ideas for using persuasive language in decision-making based on fairly factual material.

■ **Time capsule.** What ten things would you choose to include to give people of the future some idea of how we live today?

■ **Survival.** Imagine you were flying on an aeroplane when it crashes into a mountain one cold, dark, snowy night. You and your friend are the only survivors. You have to get away from the plane but you cannot carry much. Which five of the following things would you take to help you survive? Remember - you need to give good reasons: sunglasses, matches, length of rope, blanket, bottle of water, parachute, first-aid kit, torch, map, chocolate. When you have decided, compare your answers with another group's. Are they different? Why? Whose answers are the best?

■ **Who should be left out?** You are going on an expedition to the Antarctic. You can take only three others with you. Talk about which of these people would you take? Who wouldn't you take and why? Your reasons had better be good!

- Dr Sen - an experienced doctor.
- Jean Dobbs - a map-maker who has been to the Antarctic before.
- David Jones - a specialist in polar animals.
- Fiona Ferguson - an expert with motors.
- John Harris - a rock climber and mountaineer.
- Debbie Mason - a scientist used to working in extreme conditions.
- Eddie Carter - a photographer.

It's just a matter of opinion! Here are some ideas for using persuasive language in decision-making based on identifying the opinions of others and in stating and justifying your own.

■ Give the group two different points of view on an issue, e.g. pocket money should be given without strings; pocket money should be earned. Ask members of the group to decide which point of view they agree with and to try and persuade others in the group to agree with them.

■ Look at letters from magazines, e.g. TV magazines, expressing different viewpoints about TV programmes. Discuss the sorts of views expressed and try to imagine the sort of people who subscribe to these particular views. Lead on to a discussion of children's TV viewing and their viewpoints on particular programmes.

■ What rules are there, or should there be, for the playground? Ask pairs of children to think up five important rules and list them. Next get them in fours to compare and justify their lists and to see if they can come up with a consensually agreed list of five between them.

■ Preparing and giving a short talk to the class is one way of encouraging children to think about and use persuasive language. Ask them to think of something they are particularly interested in, or feel strongly about. Ask them to talk about the subject (to inform others), but at the same time to try and persuade others that this is a good thing to do or believe, etc.

Moral dilemmas! Here are some ideas for using persuasive language in decision-making based on choosing the best option from a range of choices in situations presenting possible moral dilemmas.

■ You are in a shop and you see an old lady put a packet of tea into her bag without paying for it. She looks very poor. What should you do?

■ You are on holiday. Your parents have told you not to go too far because the tide is coming in. You go for a walk around the bay and suddenly you realise you are stranded. You cannot get back to your parents because you are cut off by the incoming tide. What should you do?

ADVERTISING

- In advertising someone is always trying to influence, persuade and change our thinking.

Probably one of the most pervasive uses of persuasive language is advertising. We are bombarded with it in the newspapers and magazines, on hoardings, on radio and TV and so on. Advertising is often subtle and almost subliminal in many cases. Do children appreciate what is going on? What advertisers are trying to do?

Before dealing with this topic it is important that we appreciate what advertising attempts to do. Most advertising can be summarised by this principle: 'Find out what the people out there really want in life - and then make them believe that whatever we want to sell them will give it to them.'

Here is a list of many of these 'dreams'. You will find them time and again in all kinds of advertising:

✓ a happy family life
✓ a successful career
✓ luxury
✓ wealth
✓ good looks
✓ masculinity (men) and femininity (women)
✓ the sellers of products care about us
✓ buying this product will make us one of a select number.

Favourite adverts. Get children to discuss their favourite adverts. Ask them to explain what they like about them. Get them to give their opinions on a range of adverts and to rank them and justify their thinking. Perhaps you could carry out a survey of class favourites and discuss these.

■ **Analysing adverts.** Collect together a variety of adverts from magazines and newspapers. Discuss the products being advertised and the actual advertisements themselves. What are the adverts trying to sell you? How are they doing it? Consider what methods are being used to promote the product. Appealing to a sense of humour? Making life easier? Consider the advertiser's strategies and how successful you think they are. Do the advertisements appeal to certain kinds of people, e.g. the young, the active, etc.? Which adverts do you think are most successful and why? Do the adverts tell you much about the actual product itself?

Persuasive language in adverts. Words are an important part of advertising technique and children can learn much about persuasive language. What sorts of words do advertisers use? Are visual images or pictures more important? What sort of things don't advertisers tell you? Are they always accurate and truthful?

■ **Complaints.** If a product is not all it has been advertised as, how do you complain about it? This can involve discussion of writing letters and role-play involving negotiation skills.

As a follow up to this, children can work in pairs with an aim to developing an advertising campaign for a particular new product, e.g. a chocolate bar, a new aftershave. They will need to reflect on all they have learned:

- target audience
- style of advert
- wording
- visuals
- use of colour
- page layout.

■ *They should work on and actually produce their advertisement and present it to the rest of the class. This can be more fun if groups choose a TV advert! The group needs to explain the thinking behind the campaign to tell the others what they were trying to achieve. The audience can then tell them if they have been successful, bringing out the value of critical comment.*

Other things that are worth noticing in the way you are being manipulated are the stress on the following in advertisements:

- ✔ science, progress, jargon,
- ✔ new products all the time
- ✔ the use of superlatives
- ✔ flattery
- ✔ gimmicks
- ✔ babies
- ✔ young animals
- ✔ and many more!

FOR SALE

NICE BIG HOUSE
£130,000

LISTENING AS A SKILL

Speaking and listening are interrelated and integral skills. The fact that this section is at the back of this book and only covers two pages is not indicative of the value placed upon listening as a skill. The small group situations appropriate for the activities and suggestions in this book are designed to encourage the development of responsive and active listening skills too. Separate activities are not therefore suggested but the following notes bring out the important points.

● Listening involves:
- paying attention
- understanding,
  following and
  remembering
- responding.

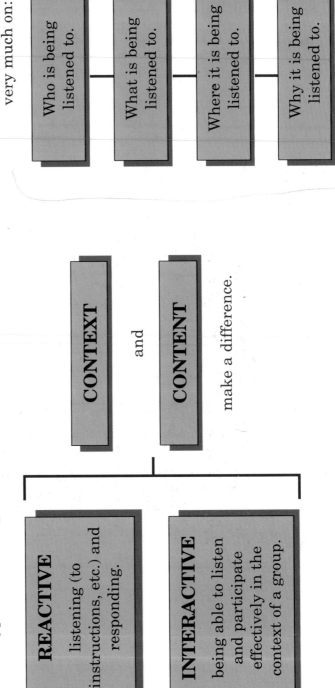

How well we listen depends very much on:

- Who is being listened to.
- What is being listened to.
- Where it is being listened to.
- Why it is being listened to.

The two types of listening dealt with in this book are:

CONTEXT

and

CONTENT

make a difference.

REACTIVE
listening (to instructions, etc.) and responding.

INTERACTIVE
being able to listen and participate effectively in the context of a group.

Children tend to listen better if the information or content of what is spoken is relevant, meaningful, interesting or important to them personally.

■ It is helpful if they know what their role is and how and when they are expected to make a response.

■ It is important to try and involve them in situations, e.g. in story time inviting responses by asking questions like 'What do you think happens next?'

■ Children should be encouraged to ask questions and clarify things they don't understand.

■ They should be encouraged to remember, retell, recite information in their own words and to relate it to their own experiences.

In group situations children need to be able to:

- *understand turn-taking and the timing of contributions*
- *know how to listen and give weight to others' contributions*
- *be able to disagree courteously*
- *be able to adjust and adapt to views expressed*
- *be able to respond to talk in different contexts for different purposes*
- *be able to gain and hold attention of others*
- *be able to listen attentively for a sustained period.*

ACKNOWLEDGEMENTS

Photography by James and Duncan of Stills except where stated.

Our thanks to the staff and children of Hilborough Junior School, Luton.

Other photography by Val Cliff on pages 4, 6, 7, 17, 18, 72, 73.

Photographs from Picturepoint - London on pages 5, 8, 22, 52.

Photograph from Robert Harding Picture Library on page 92.

Illustration by Valeria Petrone and children involved in the project, especially Andrea Gee.

Cover design by Sandra Buchanan Design Associates.

The publishers would like to thank the following for permission to reproduce material:

Spike Milligan Productions Limited for *The Gofongo* and its illustration from *A Book of Milliganimals*, Puffin Books 1968.

The Australian Tourist Commission.

Blackie and Sons and Jonathan Cape and The Bodley Head for material from their catalogues, 32 to 36.

Jillian Luff of Bitmap Graphics for the map extract on page 46.

The Jabberwock engraving designed by Sir John Tenniel.

The publishers have made every effort to contact copyright holders but this has not always been possible. If any have been overlooked we will be pleased to make any necessary arrangements.